Winners Are Big Tippers

Winners Are Big Tippers

a novel by
jim bausch

Pentland Press, Inc.
www.pentlandpressusa.com

James Bausch has been a proven leader and organizer in the Teamster Movement. This photo was taken when he was running for Secretary-Treasurer within the organization. He served as Shop Steward for Old Consolidated Motor Lines and Associated Transport, and for Canny Trucking Co. He was also a powerful speaker in regards to a member's Voice, Choice and Vote.

PUBLISHED BY PENTLAND PRESS, INC.
5122 Bur Oak Circle, Raleigh, North Carolina 27612
United States of America
919-782-0281

ISBN 1-57197-270-6
Library of Congress Control Number: 00-136682

Copyright © 2001 Jim Bausch
All rights reserved, which includes the right to reproduce this book or portions thereof in any form whatsoever except as provided by the U.S. Copyright Law.

Printed in the United States of America

Dedicated in memory of my wife, Mae.

Her name was Mary, Mary grand as any name can be.
In society with propriety they say "Marie."
Her name was Mary, Mary long before the fashions came,
And there is something there that sounds so square.
It's a grand old name.

Introduction

There was a guy who went to confession. He told the priest that he stole twenty thousand pounds of lumber.

The priest asked, "You what?"

"I stole twenty thousand pounds of lumber."

The priest asked, "What did you do with all that lumber?"

The guy told him that he had built a two-room bungalow. The priest said, "My, oh my! This is certainly one for the books.

"Well," the priest said, "for your penance, I want you to make a novena."

The guy said, "Okay, Father, how many rooms is that? I have plenty of lumber left."

Chapter

The year was 1926 and Jim was seven years old. Jim was the youngest of five children. His father was a longshoreman who worked on most of the piers on the west side waterfront. Jim's mother took good care of the house and her children. They lived in an apartment on the lower West side known as Chelsea. It was located between Greenwich Village and Hell's Kitchen. Their apartment was always clean and there was always good food on the table.

Like other families before, during and after the depression, they had their ups and downs. The school that the children attended was on the same block where they lived and it was very easy for them, especially during the cold winters, to get to school.

Jim was a well-behaved boy except on school mornings. His mother, with the help of his older brothers and sisters, would have to practically drag Jim to school on many occasions.

In spite of his hatred for school, Jim knew one thing and knew it well. He knew how to count. This was true of all the kids on the west side. The one thing they all loved to do and could do well was playing cards, shoot crap and pitch pennies. They all loved to gamble, even while playing marbles or bottle caps. They always played for keeps and got into many fights over their games with each other.

At seven years old, Jim already knew the odds in shooting craps. All the kids would hustle a few cents doing chores. They would chop wood, carry coal and even go down to the train yards for ice for anyone who would give them a nickel or a dime. The money would either be spent in a candy store or a card or crap game. The kids loved to play banker, broker, poker and six or seven card Rummy.

The older kids all did well in school. Everyone did their homework except Jim. He was always looking for an excuse to get out of homework and studying. All he ever wanted to do was play with his friends.

Summer, of course, was their best time of the year. There was no school and the children could play all day. They played stickball, handball, checkers and they skated. When someone turned the pump on, kids would have a grand time washing themselves and splashing under the pump.

There weren't many of the neighborhood kids who could swim. Most just went into water up to their waists at the local pools located in the high schools or public schools. They would dive off the docks and hang off the pilings under the piers. When the tide was low, the water was filthy. All sorts of waste gathered right at the end of the sewer. They thought nothing of diving right in, pushing the slop out of the way and laughing at it all.

The winters were bitter. School janitors, building superintendents and shop keepers had to shovel the sidewalks. Sometimes the snow was so high on both sides of the street that a trench would be dug in front of most stores so that people could cross from one side of the street to the other.

When Jim and his friends got tired of the snow and sleigh riding, and there was no place else to go, they would go into the cellar of one of the tenements. Woodsheds were used as storerooms for the tenants to keep old trunks or old furniture. Extra coal and wood was also stored there for use in the coal stoves in their apartments. There were no lights in these storerooms, so Jim and his friends would always find an old plumbing candle to light and then set up a card game.

They used an old trunk for their table and with the light from the candle, they dealt out the cards. The candle was knocked over plenty of times and there was always danger of a bad fire. The janitors would often chase them out of the cellar as soon as they heard the hollering and fighting that always went on during their card or crap games.

Jim and his friends had another interesting pastime in the basements. They would locate the biggest cobweb they could find and each boy would then capture a fly and put it in the cobweb. They would then bet that their fly would be the one the spider would eat first. They weren't being cruel. To them that was the way of life.

Jim's family had a nice apartment in the building. Theirs was one of the few on the block that had a bathroom. In most apartments, toilets were in the hall and the bathtub was in the kitchen. Some houses still had toilets in the yard. It was always a laugh to all the kids to see who had to take their potty in the morning in the backyard outhouse.

Chapter

The days, weeks, months and years passed quickly. The day finally arrived for Jim to finish grade school. The only thing that he wanted to do was get a job and make some money. In those days work was not easy to find. The fruit and vegetable peddlers were about the only people who would look for a kid to work for them. They paid a dollar a day. That was mostly on Saturdays, from very early in the morning until about 6 P.M. The customers would call out their windows and holler down to the peddlers to tell them what they wanted. Five pounds of potatoes, a head of cabbage, and so on. Then, the boys would run up the stairs and make the delivery. Sometimes they received a nickel tip. By the end of the day, they might end up with a dollar pay and a dollar in tips. Other jobs were working in local stores, running errands and making deliveries. These jobs only paid three or four dollars a week.

One day, Jim learned about being a mutt. A mutt delivered telegrams for Western Union. Western Union boys had to wear mustard colored khaki uniforms. Whenever a mutt came around on their own block, the other kids would razz them. They laughed because they were envious. A mutt could earn $15 a week including tips. Not bad for a kid in those days. Jim lasted eight months on the Western Union job and then quit.

After Jim left Western Union, he got a job at the local meat, fruit and vegetable market. He did his job very well. The tips were pretty good and the boss even started to teach Jim how to cut meat and clean the chickens.

By the time that Jim was sixteen, he was doing very well at the market. He started to notice a very pretty girl who came into the market to shop with her mother. He overheard his boss call the girl Mary. Jim always made it his business to wait on them as soon as he saw them come in. He was trying to impress Mary and her mother.

Mary also noticed Jim at the market. It was not hard to notice him. He always went out of his way for her and her mom. He would take their orders for meat ahead of all the other people waiting to be served. He would pick out the freshest vegetables and the ripest fruits.

Mary had talked about Jim for months to her friends. Dotty and Anne had been friends with Mary since grade school. They would laugh and tease her about her eating more just so she could go shopping again and see Jim. Mary had never dated before and was really shy. She had a good head on her shoulders and knew what she wanted in life. She wanted to meet a great man, get married and have several children and a house with a white picket fence.

Mary's family did not have much money, but that never kept her from meeting Dotty and Anne on the weekends to shop at Macy's. She loved just getting together with the girls. They would hit the stores as soon as they opened and go straight to the ladies' department. They would find an item that they knew they wanted and watch it for weeks until it was marked down to a price that they could afford. Mary was frugal, but she always managed to get what she wanted.

After Macy's the girls would head over to the coffee shop and talk about everything that happened in their lives that week. Dotty would talk about her boyfriend, Anne would talk about her new husband and Mary would talk about Jim.

When Jim got the chance, he asked Mary to go to the movies with him and the ice cream parlor afterwards. She asked permission from her mother who said it would be all right, but that she could not be out late.

Jim and Mary became great friends. They always talked about all kinds of things and their plans. Jim always told Mary how he remembered the hard times, the bread lines, the guys selling apples on the corners for a nickel each. Jim told her how the kids would sell the *New York Daily News* and the *Daily Mirror* at night. They'd go up to Penn Station where the newspaper trucks dropped the papers off. The drivers sold them seven *News'* and seven *Mirror's* for twenty cents. They were seven for a dime. The kids then sold them for five cents, which meant they each made seventy cents, a fifty-cent profit. Sometimes they would include the *New York American* that came out in the mornings. Those papers were three for a nickel, sold for five cents, and they made a profit of ten cents.

Jim told all this to Mary and all about his exploits to earn some money. But Jim hadn't told Mary how he liked to gamble, play cards, shoot dice, play the numbers and even a horse once in a while. He kept these things to himself. Jim loved to think that he was such a wise guy, between his pay, the few tips he made and his luck at cards and dice, he always seemed to have a few extra bucks. He loved treating Mary to extra special shows and movies and ice cream at the corner ice cream parlor. Once in a while, instead of taking the bus or subway, Jim would hail a cab to get to the movies or go home. On Sunday nights they would go to local Parish halls where they would watch basketball games or attend dances, all for just twenty-five cents admission. They were lucky. Many poor guys didn't have the twenty-five cents.

Mary started working at the telephone company as a switchboard operator. Many of Jim's friends were working on the docks as longshoremen. Jim knew all about the docks from his father and he knew that for those who worked fairly steady, the money was pretty good.

With the money Mary was making at the telephone company, she was now able to buy more things on her weekend outings. Dating Jim had brought her such happiness and gave her so much more to talk about on her trips with her friends.

Mary would tell them in detail her plans for the future. Jim knew how to treat a lady and so she knew she would have a good life. They really enjoyed each other's company and Jim always showed her a good time. He was always surprising her by bringing her to shows and always had money in his pocket.

By this time, Anne was a mother and was often envious of Mary's life with Jim, but still loved to hear the stories about their dates. Mary would glow as she talked about the dances and games she went to. She would brag about Jim and how he always brought a flower for her when he picked her up for dates.

Eventually, Anne had another child and stopped meeting the girls for their weekend outings. Mary and Dotty made a pact that they would never stop meeting even after they married and had children.

Chapter 3

Jim's friends convinced him to come down to the waterfront and look for work there. Jim told them he'd try it. He knew that he could join the union and make more money than he was making at the meat market. Someone pointed out to the hiring boss that Jim was one of the neighbors' sons. It always helped to have a connection, and between his friends and his father, Jim was hired and started to do well.

There were many days when there were no ships in port and that simply meant no work and no pay.

Another year passed and Jim was doing well financially. Things started to look much better for Jim and now he and Mae, as he called Mary, started to think of marriage.

At the age of twenty, Jim married Mary, who was nineteen. They chose an apartment in the tenement next to Jim's family. They bought most of their furniture from a local store on 8th Avenue, where most of the people in the neighborhood of Chelsea and Greenwich Village bought their furniture.

Right after their first year of marriage, their first child was born. Jim was so proud of their beautiful baby girl. Her name was Dolly. Jim could hardly wait to come home from the docks at night to see and hold Dolly. He was the happiest father in town.

Mary took to motherhood well. She doted on Dolly and loved dressing her up in cute little dresses and adorable hats. Mary would take Dolly with her on weekends to shop with Dotty. She was a very good baby and so taking her everywhere was not a problem.

Shortly after Dolly was born, Dotty had a child of her own. Mary would bring Dolly and Dotty would bring her son. They would spend the mornings at the park and the afternoons at Macy's. The children would nap in their carriages while their mothers shopped.

Mary was happy. She had a loving husband and a beautiful baby girl. Mary couldn't help but think of what a lucky woman she was. But of course, sometimes happiness is not total.

Jim was working steadily on the docks now. Although he'd come home directly from the Pier's he would sometimes take two hours to get home. It seems there was a washroom, toilet and a dirty old locker room at the head of the dock. Few guys ever really used the room for those purposes, but there was always a crap game or card game going on in there. The dock bosses would have to get the longshoremen away from the gambling and back to work. It was the same with the truck drivers who were there on the shipping line, also known as the delivery line, where drivers picked up freight from the pier.

One night Jim, several truck drivers and longshoremen were in the room, as usual, shooting dice and playing poker. Suddenly, the cops surrounded the room. No one was allowed in or out. Two paddy wagons were backed up to the doors and everyone was locked up, including Jim.

They were held at the local precinct until it was time to go to night court. The judge let them all go, but not before he gave them a stern warning. He told them that their jobs were on the line and if he saw any of them in front of him again, it would mean at least ten days in lock-up for them.

Jim arrived home about eleven o'clock where he found Mae waiting for him.

"Well, are you satisfied?" Mae asked.

"Yeah, I know," Jim answered.

"Suppose they put someone else in your gang on the pier and you have to start the shape-up again," Mae said.

"We'll see in the morning," Jim told her.

After the dock boss blew the whistle at 8 A.M. the next morning for the gangs to check into the pier and get to work, he told them loud and clear that they'd better not let it happen again, or else they could take a walk.

A few days after that incident, Jim and Mae settled down to their routine and he was back to normal.

Chapter

When the war effort started to build for World War II, Mae was pregnant with their second child. As happy as they were about their expected new child, there was bad news too. Mae's mother became ill and died. Her father had died when Mae was a young child. Their second daughter, Nancy, was welcomed into the world, offsetting their grief.

When the war began, Jim received his draft notice for induction. He served over three years. While he was home on furlough, Mae became pregnant with their third child, another girl they named Susan.

When Nancy was born, Mary and Jim were still able to make due but times really got hard when Jim was away. Jim's allotment barely covered their food and rent. Mae had to give up her weekends with her friend. They had made a pact that they would never do that and Mae had to break her promise. She felt terrible about doing it, but Dotty was a good friend and she understood.

When the war ended, Jim was anxious to return to work on the docks. Bills had piled up since all Mae and the children had to live on was his allotment from his service pay.

Getting back to work was great. The money was good and the bills got paid. The children were growing fast and before they knew it, Dolly was ready for first grade. They were one big happy family.

Jim would tell the guys on the pier about the card games and crap games he played while in the service and the guys told him about the games they played.

"Let me tell you about this one guy," Jim told them. "He was a sergeant named Brown. He came from Chicago. Boy, was he sharp. Real clever. If he got off to a bad start, he would just quit for the day." He went on to tell them he'd just wait until the next day, have a fresh start, do well, and was able to send money home to his family.

For the most part, Jim just watched the guys gamble while he was in the Army. Jim never had any money, not after taking care of his family back in the States. He had too little and it was too risky to get into games with no money and soldiers who seemed to be as good as real professional gamblers.

Back home, he would occasionally play the numbers or get into a card or dice game. Jim felt that one day he'd score a big one. The local social club on 9th Avenue was one of his favorite hangouts. If the weather was nice on a Saturday afternoon or an evening during the week, he'd sit in on a poker game at the club. He won a few and lost a few, but never much to speak of. He was always glad to meet and talk to guys that he'd known for years. There were all kinds of characters that hung around the club and lots of wise guys. Jim could not help but hear some of them plotting a stick up, something about a payroll. These guys were just out for a fast buck. None of them ever seemed to have a job, but were always well dressed and had plenty of money.

The years were going by pretty fast and the kids were getting older. Before they knew it, Dolly was talking about her graduation. Jim could hardly believe it.

"I guess it won't be long before they'll be having boyfriends and then making plans to get married," Jim said to Mae.

Jim and Mae never had much in the way of possessions and never took a real vacation. The most they ever did was spend a night down at Midland Beach in Staten Island at friend's house or visited relatives down in Rockaway. The kids loved the beach. Once in a while, they would pack a nice lunch and go on a day trip on the Hudson River Day Line up to Bear Mountain.

On the docks, Jim had made a lot of headway. He had started to drive a hi lo forklift. In the beginning, he dropped several loads of freight, some of them over the side of the dock. But eventually, he became an expert with the hi lo.

Just as Jim had predicted, the girls began bringing boyfriends home, and before long, all three girls had married. After the girls were settled in their own homes with their new husbands, the house got very quiet with just Jim and Mae there.

Jim often got into a crap game or poker game at work. On occasion, he played a game called the tossing game. The tossing game was when someone would have a flat stick about a foot long. He'd put two pennies on the stick, one heads-up and the other tails-up. Players in the game bet odds or even. When all the bets were down, the person would toss the pennies up into the air and, the way that they landed depended on who collected or who paid off. It was a fast gambling game. Guys lost their pay in five or ten minutes and then went home broke, or visited a loan shark to get some money. They were then forced to pay off the loan shark each week. These guys always seemed to owe somebody something, and sometimes they'd hock their rings, watches and even their clothes.

Jim was taken twice in the tossing game. He was lucky that Mae was able to handle buying the food and paying the bills until his next pay day and that he never had to visit a loan shark.

When the guys went broke, they knew no other way to raise money except to go to pawn brokers or loan sharks. Many of the guys lived alone in furnished rooms and had to have their rent paid on Saturday or they had to leave.

One after the other, Jim and Mae's children had children of their own. They were proud of their children and doted on their grandchildren. They were happy that their daughters all had married nice, hard-working men and that they all lived close by. One daughter lived in the Bronx, another in Brooklyn and one in Queens. Jim and Mae took the subway for visits, birthdays, christenings and holidays. Before they knew it, their grandchildren were ready and anxious to go to school. They weren't like Jim who had hated school. Jim was very proud of them all.

Jim started to think about retirement. He and Mae knew friends and neighbors who'd retired and all seemed to be doing okay. They had Social Security and pensions from their jobs. Jim and Mae talked it over. Should they try to set a day or a time and just put in for retirement? They bounced this back and forth and talked it over with their kids. The kids all told Jim to retire.

"Yeah, but if I retire, what would we do? We don't have a country home, or even a place in Florida. For years, those places were so cheap. When that guy who used to be on television said 'Come on down', we knew that it sounded good, but we never really had any money. We were always glad to just pay our bills and have good food on the table," Jim told them. "I guess that is about all we wanted. Of course," he added, "if I'd stayed away from crap games and poker and playing the numbers, even the horses once in a while, then I guess we might have had a few dollars in the bank."

His youngest daughter said, "Pop, however little you played cards or anything else, you deserved it. So don't worry about it."

"Do you mean that I deserved to lose?"

She laughed. "No, Pop. You know what I mean. Furthermore, I do think it would be very nice if you and Mom really look into buying a small place down in Florida. And once in a while, we could go down for a visit."

"Yes," Jim agreed. "That would be nice and we could even come up and visit all of you."

Everyone was agreeing at once on what a great idea it was for them to retire and move to Florida.

"Maybe I could work through the coming spring and summer and then retire before winter," Jim said. "That way, there would be no more getting out on those cold winter mornings. In the meantime, we can keep our eyes open for ads in the papers about places in Florida."

Chapter

Weeks and months went by and soon the time came for Jim to retire. The winters were cold and it was so good for Jim to be able to stay in bed late and have a late breakfast. He and Mae would go out for walks once in a while or to the stores. Jim would occasionally drop into the club for a little poker and to talk with his old friends. Jim and Mae watched television a lot, especially old movies that ran until late into the night. They were starting to really enjoy their time together. Every now and then, Mae would invite old friends over for dinner. In the meantime, Jim was playing lotto and waiting for the day when he would hit it big. But it always seemed like he had no luck.

"You know," Jim said to Mae, "trying to hit the lotto is like trying to hit the Irish Sweepstakes. Do you remember how I used to buy and then sell Irish Sweepstakes tickets, but we never hit? I always thought that sooner or later we would score with a big hit."

Jim had been playing the lotto since New York State started the game. At first, it was only a dollar a week on Saturdays. After a few months, with no sign of winning, Jim started playing on Monday's and Wednesday's as well. With no winning numbers, Jim began playing for an extra dollar or two on Saturday's. This went on for a few years. Jim noticed how many times he would have two or three numbers of the winning ticket, and this pattern continued for another year.

Jim then thought he had a plan to win. He noticed that many times he had three numbers in one slot and the balance of the six numbers needed to win lotto in the other slots. So now what to do? Why not pick out all the numbers that he wanted to play and then put them in a box, shake them up and pick out six numbers needed to win lotto. At first, he played three dollars worth on Saturday. Again he came close, but never more than three numbers in any one slot. Now he saw that there was only one thing to do. Why not play a full card for five dollars, using the same method? He kept coming close, but not winning. On two occasions while watching the lotto numbers being picked on Saturday night television, he had the first three numbers picked both times. He thought for sure that he would be a winner.

This went on for almost five years until finally, one Saturday, he had four numbers, including the supplementary number. Now Jim felt great. He finally had broken the ice and thought for sure that he had the right formula to win the lotto.

Now he would play a full card only on Saturdays for five dollars. Again, he always picked the numbers out of a box, always played all the family birthdays. He not only played the birthdays of those who were still alive, he even played the birthdays of his father, mother, sister and brothers who had died. A few months of this strategy and he did hit the four number slot two different times. That meant that Jim hit three times in all. He figured that he was out about five hundred dollars. A guy had once told him that a good way to hit lotto was to pick his three favorite numbers and just add three numbers and maybe he'd come up a winner.

That method did not do Jim much good either. He noticed that he would have the six numbers but he did not have them together. He just kept playing and trying because he kept telling himself, if you are not in it, you cannot win it.

He was saving a lot of these five-dollar cards that were full of numbers and now had about ten full cards. He thought, why not play two full cards. That would be ten dollars. Again, he had a few close calls, but no winners. He came up with the idea to play four full cards for twenty dollars just on Saturdays. Jim struck out again and decided to go for fifty dollars and play all of the full cards that he had. He went for this action three times, only on Saturdays. Still no luck.

Jim started to wonder what he would do if he ever did hit the six numbers. What would be the best thing to do? Consult a lawyer? Talk to an accountant? Maybe include a few members of the family in as partners of a winning ticket? He could always see himself on television being interviewed. Would he make any trips? Go on a cruise? Buy a house, a new car, or donate to charity? Well, of course, Jim had to think of all of the angles just in case he won so that he would not look like such a dummy, all flustered and not knowing what to say. He had many nice dreams about the things that he would do and the places that he would see.

It was late in the afternoon and Jim and Mae were enjoying a quiet, relaxing evening. While Jim read the paper, Mae began to prepare supper. Suddenly, the phone rang and it was Dolly from Brooklyn. She was hysterical on the other end of the phone and Mae could not understand her through her sobs. Finally, Mae was able to make out what Dolly was saying. A car had just hit Dolly's youngest daughter, Mary. Jim could tell that something was seriously wrong and grabbed the phone from Mae.

"How is Mary? Is she okay?"

"No Pop, she's not. She's in the emergency room right now and it looks serious."

"Mom and I will be right there! Do you need us to call anyone?"

"Would you please? I just got home from work and I haven't been able to leave Mary's side since."

"No problem," replied Jim. "Try and stay calm. I'll take care of everything."

After calling the girls, Jim and Mae were out of the house and at the hospital within the hour.

Dolly was in with the doctor when they arrived, but was soon able to explain what had happened. Apparently some young guy had been driving by and it looked like he was showing off in front of the kids when suddenly, he got too close to the curb and his front wheel went up on the sidewalk and hit Mary. She went flying up into the air and crashed on the hood of the car. All of the kids in the neighborhood were screaming and several people had gathered around to help. When the cops finally arrived, they had to push men away from the driver, afraid that they wanted to hurt him.

In the meantime, everyone had arrived at the hospital. Nancy and Bill with their children and Susan and Dave with all of theirs. Kitty was finally starting to calm down. She had been hysterical since the accident. After all, Mary was her best friend and she was right there when the accident occurred. So there they were, all sitting in the waiting room hardly talking, but surely praying that Mary would be okay.

Hours had gone by when the doctor finally came into the waiting room and told all of them that Mary was asleep. Her right leg was broken and put into a cast while the other was just badly bruised. She was in a lot of pain, but ultimately they thought she'd be okay. The doctor told them all to go home and get some rest.

On their way home, Jim and Mae felt a bit of relief knowing that Mary would be okay. They also realized what a wonderfully supportive family they had and knew that they had been blessed.

The next day Jim and Mae visited the hospital again. Dolly and Ed were there and things looked much better. Mary was playing with her doll and talking. You could tell she was feeling better. The doctor came into the room and was pleased with Mary's condition. He told Dolly and Ed that they would be able to take Mary home in a day or two. Everyone was relieved to hear the doctor say those words. After a month or two, the doctor took Mary's cast off and in no time she was up and running with Kitty and the rest of the kids.

Chapter

The year was 1990. Jim had been playing lotto on Saturdays for about six months, and had been playing all ten cards for fifty dollars. Now he went back to one full card for five dollars. One Sunday morning, he was looking at the *New York Post* to get Saturday's results of the lotto. He knew his favorite numbers by heart. His heart jumped. There was 5, 12, 18, 23, 30, and 31. He looked again and really started to shake. He got his tickets and there it was, the same numbers. "I have it! I got it! Am I looking at this straight? Is this right?" He ran in to wake up his wife and kept hollering, "We won! We won! We hit the lotto! We are rich!" They were laughing, shouting and crying—everybody must have heard. He seriously hoped not everyone heard since he knew enough to keep this quiet.

Jim and Mae were holding on to each other. They were very excited. Mae said she had to call the kids to let them know about their good luck.

"No, no," Jim said. "The first thing I want to do is look at my lotto ticket and make sure it's a winner. We have to put the ticket in a safe place and for now, do not tell anyone about winning. Let's just take it real easy and try to stay calm," he told Mae. "Nobody must know about this for now."

They were both so excited that they could not have their usual pancake and sausage Sunday breakfast. They just drank coffee all morning. They talked about a hundred different things to do. Jim kept saying that they would tell no one. They could not concentrate on the Sunday papers, television, or anything else.

Jim told Mae that he would talk to a lawyer to see if there was any way of getting out of paying some of the taxes. Mae suggested that he talk to an accountant to see if he could give them some advice.

"The first thing you should do, Jim," Mae said, "is sign the back of the winning ticket and put it in a safety deposit box at the bank until we are sure of what to do."

Later in the day, after much thought, Jim said to his wife, "You know, you gave me an idea when you said to put the ticket in a safe deposit box at the bank. I am thinking of going to a bank, but instead of putting the ticket in a safe deposit box, asking the bank if I can get a loan, up front, on the strength of the value of the ticket. In other words, the state pays off one payment once a year for twenty years. Suppose I ask a bank to give us a loan, using the ticket for collateral. Let's try to figure this out," he told Mae.

"The winning ticket is worth four million dollars. Now, after taxes, maybe about $2,500,000 over a twenty-year span. What we have to do is figure out just how much money per year we would get at one payment a year. Then, based on that amount, maybe we can get a bank to give us a loan, say at twelve percent interest, the same as they would charge for someone who wants to buy a house and pay off a twenty year mortgage."

"Do you think a bank would be that interested?" Mae asked.

"Why not? And what have we got to lose by asking? The money is good. It should be better than just trying to pay off a loan or a mortgage working on a straight salary. In other words, the money will be coming from the state, as good as gold, and as sure as day and night."

"Well," Mae said, "I guess it would be worth a try."

It was settled. Tomorrow, Jim would go to a bank, ask a few questions and see what they had to say.

"But one other thing," Jim said. "We will not be able to sign the back of the lotto ticket because if a bank should be interested, the ticket would have to be clear so that they will be able to put an official name on the ticket."

For the rest of that Sunday, Jim and Mae went over idea after idea on what to do and places to go. They wanted to help the rest of the family with their bills, the grandchildren's' education, relatives who they knew could use a little help and contribute to their church and charities. They thought about where they would like to move, buy a house and a new car. They talked about all the good things that everyone would like to do and see. It was a very happy night.

After the late night news, Jim and Mae finally went to bed. Jim was still thinking as he lay there trying to sleep. He thought that he would go to the bank where they had their savings account. They knew a few of the people there and had been using that bank for years. He had gone over and over in his mind just what he would ask the bank. Finally, he fell asleep.

He awoke, thinking it was six o'clock. Glancing at the alarm clock, the clock read 4:45 A.M. Jim just lay there thinking. He tried to push the thoughts out of his head, relax and go back to sleep. Hearing the 6 A.M. alarm tick, Jim decided he'd better get up.

Mae heard him get up so she arose also. She asked him what time it was. She told Jim that he had been keeping her awake, tossing and turning all night and suggested that they try to go back to sleep because they couldn't do anything until later on.

"I can't sleep," he told her. "I must have been thinking all night, even if I did doze off. I must have still been trying to think. I'll put the coffee on and read the paper awhile."

"As long as you want to talk to someone at the bank," she said, "I think you should go about 10 A.M. That way, someone who can answer your questions will be in the office. Suppose the bank lets it be known that we are lotto winners even if they are not interested in your idea of buying the ticket from us."

"When I go to the bank, I will ask to see someone in charge of the loan department and tell them that my business must be kept confidential. I won't take the ticket with me. I'll just ask if they would be interested in buying the ticket from me or giving me a loan, letting the ticket pay off the loan once a year for twenty years."

Jim and Mae settled at the table with a breakfast of cereal and coffee. "I was thinking," he said, "about one of the things we may be able to do. Let's get all the kids and grandchildren together and go up to the Poconos for a full week, or even two weeks. We could have a load of fun."

"Right away? How can everybody get off from work at the same time?" Mae asked.

"Why not? All of them have pretty good jobs and lots of seniority, and we could just work it out. We cannot wait until the summer is over. We have to plan early, like April or maybe even earlier. Of course, it's just a thought," he said. "I'd like to look into it because I do think that we could have a lot of fun all being together like that."

Jim constantly watched the clock. Mae tried telling Jim to take it easy and not to get too excited. He assured her he was okay because, as he said, "One way or the other, the money is ours." When he asked her if she wanted to go to the bank with him, she told him she didn't.

"I'll stay here, straighten up the house and wait until you come back. You are only going to look for some information right now. We can talk more when we know what they have to say."

Jim agreed. It wasn't even 8 A.M., but Jim went in to get ready for his trip to the bank.

By 9 A.M., Jim had been ready and pacing the floor, waiting for the time to pass so he could walk to the bank. He thought that no matter what the bank said, he would check with one or two other banks just to see if he could get a better deal.

Chapter

When he reached the bank where they had their account, one of the women asked if she could help him.

"Yes. I'd like to see someone about a loan," he said.

"Take a seat," she told him. "Mr. Jones will be right with you."

A few minutes later, Jones came out of his office and greeted Jim.

"I'd like to talk about a loan," Jim said.

"Come right into my office," Jones said warmly. When they were settled in Jones's office, Jones asked, "How much money would you like to borrow?"

"First of all," Jim said, "I want you to know that my wife and I have an account in this bank."

Jones nodded. "Now, how can I be of help?"

"Here's the deal," Jim said. "We do not really need a loan, but what I am going to tell you must be kept strictly confidential."

Jones looked at him, clearly getting uneasy. "Of course. It will be a private matter. We do not discuss anyone's banking business. What is it?"

"Here's the deal," Jim repeated. "I hit the lotto over the weekend and I understand that it is for four million dollars."

Jones almost fell out of his seat in his shock and excitement. "How can we help?" he asked again, leaning forward in his seat.

"I want to save as much on the taxes as I can and was wondering if I can get enough money as possible up front instead of waiting twenty years to collect. In other words, I figure I will collect about $160,000 a year for twenty years. If I could have all the money that I can get, I could do a lot more now. I need to pay bills. I would like to pay off some of my children's mortgages, buy a house for my wife and I, and a few other things," Jim explained. "The way I see it, if all I can get is $160,000 now, I'll have to wait until next year before getting the next $160,000. This way, I figure that I could pay off all this stuff and do a lot more with all this money up front, even put a lot of money into a savings account and CDs."

Jones was looking at Jim in complete wonder. "But what is it that you would like us to do?"

"I was wondering if the bank could do one of two things. First, would the bank be interested in buying the ticket from me?"

Jones started to laugh. "No, the bank would not be interested in buying your lotto ticket. What else is there that we can help you with?"

"Is it possible that we can get a loan using the ticket for collateral?" Jim asked. "I figure that the ticket is worth $3,200,000 over a twenty-year span. How would it be if the bank gave me a loan for that amount at ten percent? That means that the bank would take out about $320,000 for the interest, giving me a balance of $2,880,000.

Jones looked at Jim, spellbound. He burst out laughing. Composing himself finally, he said, "Jim, it's a great idea if you can swing it, but I'm sure that this bank would not be interested. Of course," he told Jim, "I cannot say that for all banks, but I do not think that you can get such a loan in such a way. I feel that the bank will say it is just like gambling." He repeated again that he did not think this bank or any other bank would be interested in such a plan.

Jim rose from his seat. "Fine. I'll shop around and see what else I can come up with."

"I'd love to know," Jones said. "Good luck."

It was now 10:30 A.M. Jim walked out of the bank and he spotted another bank down the street. He was debating with himself. Should he go in and ask the same questions? Should he just forget it? *Well*, he said to himself, *I'm here at this bank. Let's see what they say. What do I have to lose?*

He entered the bank and asked to see someone about a loan. He went through the same routine, but the banker he spoke to shook his head no right from the start. Jim reminded him that this was very confidential. The man told him that it would certainly stay that way.

By noon, the weather had turned to drizzling rain. Jim was hungry and decided to go back home to tell his wife how he made out. He took his time walking home. On the way, he saw a few people he knew, but he did not stop to speak to anyone. He just waved hello and kept on going. When he arrived at his apartment and opened the door, Mae greeted him.

"How did you make out?" she asked anxiously.

"No good," he told her. "The banks don't seem to be interested in loaning me the money or buying the ticket."

While they ate their lunch, Mae told him that maybe he should forget the whole thing and just contact the lotto people and tell them they were the winners.

"Yeah, I guess you're right." He paused, deep in thought. "I wonder if it will be on television and they'll ask where the winner is, or if we will be located because they know where the ticket was purchased."

That night as they watched the news on television, not one word was spoken about the missing lottery winner. Jim figured that if it were twenty or thirty million, it would get a big play on television, but since it was only four million, they were not as interested. Jim and Mae just decided to keep it quiet for a while longer and keep the ticket in a safe place.

They put the ticket down under a rug in the corner of their clothes closet. "I really should sign the back of it," Jim said. "Just in case we ever get robbed and the crooks should find it. Let's just leave it under that rug and see what else we may be able to come up with."

After the news, they watched an old movie and then went to bed. They both slept late in the morning. The phone woke them up. It was one of their daughters.

"How is everything?" she asked.

"Okay," answered Mae. "We're just taking it easy. Nothing new is happening," Jim heard her say, and had to laugh. Mae and her daughter talked for a while and then she and Jim had breakfast. Jim read the paper to see if there was any mention of a lotto winner, but nothing was in the news. After breakfast, they decided to go for a walk. Wherever they went in the neighborhood, they were certain to meet people that they knew and to some people they met, they had a difficult time keeping their secret.

They arrived home in the afternoon, fixed some tea and settled down in front of the television. Later, they had dinner and relaxed until it was time for bed. They continued this routine for the next couple of weeks. They saw their children and grandchildren once in a while and talked to relatives and friends on the phone. There was still no mention to anyone about the winning lotto ticket.

One night, they were visiting their middle daughter and her family. During the conversation, their son-in-law, Bill, happened to mention that he had lunch downtown in a lower east side restaurant. He said that at the far side of the restaurant, a few hoods were sitting around paying close attention to a sharply dressed guy. One of Bill's friends asked him, "Do you know who that is?" Bill said he that he didn't know. His friend told him that was Sonny Condo, the well-known hood.

Bill told him that he recognized Sonny Condo now. Then he told Jim and Mae that for the rest of their lunch hour, groups would come into the restaurant, go right over to Condo, talk for a minute or two, and then leave. Jim asked Bill if he ever saw Condo in that place before. Bill said that it was one of the first times that he ever ate in that place so he didn't know if Condo was a frequent visitor or not.

The wheels in Jim's head started to turn. He started to wonder if there would be any chance that Sonny Condo would be interested in his lotto ticket. Of course, he would have to be more than careful if he were to get into any deal with this guy. Jim thought that if someone could come up front with the dough for the ticket, he could get all the money in one lump sum and do all the things that they always dreamed of.

A few days later, Jim made it his business to see Bill. "Bill, have you been back to the lunchroom where you saw Condo?"

"Yes," Bill answered. "A few of the guys that I work with started to get a little friendly with some of the guys who have been seen talking to Condo."

This was good news to Jim. He thought about whether he should take Bill into his confidence and blurt out just what was on his mind or if he should he take it easy and talk it over with Mae. He decided to talk to Mae first.

When they arrived home, he said, "I think I may have another angle to work on about the lotto ticket. Why not offer the same proposition to Condo that I offered to the bank?"

Mae started to fill that idea with holes. "How do you know he has that kind of money?"

"Oh, he's got it alright and I also think," he said, "if they are interested, they will come up with cash. He certainly cannot give me a check and, of course, he could never show where this money came from."

Mae started to get nervous. "I think that you're better off turning the ticket in to the lotto people before we are all sorry."

"Yes. Maybe you're right, I'll think about it." Jim said.

The more Jim thought about getting the money in one lump sum, the more he became interested in seeing if this could be done.

Many years ago, during the Depression, loan sharks on the waterfront would buy longshoreman's metal disks. They were called checks, on which there were certain numbers that would prove to the timekeeper and the paymaster just how much time in hours, days and money a longshoreman would have coming to him at the end of the week. On the waterfront, all piers used to pay in cash on Friday. As a longshoreman stood in line at the pay window, all he had to do was put in the check. The paymaster would count out whatever money he had coming to him. His pay would always include two-dollar bills. If a man had twenty-four dollars coming to him, he would get a twenty and two two-dollar bills. Many times, a guy who needed money would pawn jewelry for five or ten dollars. After getting the money from the hock shop, they would sometimes turn around and sell the pawn ticket to a loan shark for another two, three or five dollars. It was one of the simplest ways that a guy could get as much money as possible for a piece of jewelry or any other item of worth.

After much thought and consideration, Jim decided to see if anyone would be interested in buying the lotto ticket. Another week passed and he again visited his son-in-law, Bill. Six weeks had now passed since he had won the numbers. He finally decided that it was best to get Bill on the side and confide to him that he had the winning lotto ticket.

In a room by themselves, Jim told Bill about the ticket. Bill became excited immediately and congratulated his father-in-law.

Jim then told Bill what he'd been trying to do. He told Bill about having gone to two banks. He wondered if there was any other way he could sell the ticket and get the money up front rather than wait twenty years.

"I think that you are being very foolish," Bill advised. "Why kid yourself about all these other things and angles? Why not just turn in the ticket and get whatever the lotto pays once a year for twenty years. The way you are going, you might wind up losing the whole thing and then you'll be kicking yourself in the ass for trying to be so smart."

"Yes. I've thought of what can happen," Jim said, "but the more I think of getting all the cash up front, the more I like it."

"Well, what do you want me to do?" Bill asked.

Jim reminded Bill about the restaurant where Bill had seen Sonny Condo. "Do you think it might be possible to talk to one of these guys who knows Condo and see if he would be interested in my winning lotto ticket?"

"You must be nuts!" Bill said.

"I'm serious. It just might be possible that it all could work out very well. As a matter of fact, it may be in Condo's best interest. Not only would he make a good profit on the deal, but he could always use it as some way to show that he has a legitimate income."

"Why should he have to worry about a thing like that?" Bill asked.

"Whenever these guys get bagged or picked up for anything," Jim said, "one of the first questions that they are asked is where they are working. Of course, they usually have a front for an alibi like this."

Jim asked Bill to just see if he could talk to one of the guys who knew Condo. "See if he can set up a date for me and I'll go and talk to him anywhere. Tell him I will not have the winning ticket with me."

"Okay," Bill said, "if I get a chance, I will see if I can ask one of them and see what they have to say."

They joined the rest of the family for a good dinner and pleasant evening. Round numbers continued to spin around in Jim's head. Jim was starting to feel pretty good. His little idea started to look good one way or the other. Jim reminded Bill not to say anything to anyone. Either Condo would be interested or he would finally give in and turn the ticket over to the state lotto.

Chapter

A few days later, Bill called Jim on the phone. "I talked to one of Condo's friends. I think they call him Chinatown Harry. I told him that I knew a guy who had a winning lotto ticket worth $4,000,000 and asked if he knew of anyone who may be interested in buying it. Of course, I told him that the $4 million was before taxes. Chinatown Harry looked at me quite surprised and asked, 'Where the hell is this guy?' I told him that for now, we would not say who or where the winner is until some kind of arrangement is made for a sit down. So Harry said, 'Okay, let me look into it and see if there's anyone that may be interested.'

"Then Harry asked me how much dough were we talking about? I told him it would have to be over two million. He just looked at me and said 'Okay.' So, as of right now, I do not know if he will talk to Condo or maybe someone else. So that's it for now."

Jim said, "Okay, it sounds pretty good. If, by any chance, anyone approaches you, just take it easy. If worse comes to worse and if they start to punch you around or anything to find out who has the ticket or anything like that, just tell them that you are sure that the guy who has the ticket is going to turn it into the state lotto. In any event, give me a call if they want to talk."

A few more days passed. One day when the phone rang it was Bill. He said, "Yeah. It looks like Condo is interested."

"What happened?" Jim asked anxiously.

"He came into the lunchroom and Chinatown Harry came right over and sat at the table with me. In the meantime, I noticed Condo sitting at his usual table with what looked like a few hoods with him. I think I caught him looking me over. Harry said that he did talk to someone who may be interested, and he said that a meet would be set up maybe at this lunchroom. He said that he would stay in touch."

"Okay," Jim said. "Bill, tell Chinatown Harry that I would just as soon talk at the same lunchroom, because this way, it would be like I'm just meeting you for lunch."

A long week went by. Bill called Jim at night from home and said that Condo would be at the lunchroom tomorrow and for the guy with the winning ticket to come down and have a little talk.

"Okay," Jim said. "I'll come down around 12:30 P.M. I'll see you then."

"One other thing," Bill said. "Chinatown Harry said that in no way, shape or form should you or I ever call Condo 'Sonny Boy.' He said that there's a reporter on television that, whenever he has anything to say about Condo, always calls him Sonny Boy and Condo goes nuts. Condo says he's going to kick that guy's ass if it's the last thing he does. Harry says sometimes whenever Condo has to go to court, there are always a few reporters calling, 'Hey, Sonny Boy.' Harry said that Condo gets so mad. If he ever had a gun on him, he would shoot a few of them."

"Yeah, I read that a long time ago," Jim said, "that he doesn't like to be called Sonny Boy. So I will make sure that I never say anything like that. Did you tell Chinatown Harry that I would not have the winning ticket on me?"

"No," Bill said. "I forgot all about that. Is it in a safe place?"

Jim assured him that it was.

The next day, a Wednesday, Jim walked into the restaurant to meet Bill. Bill greeted Jim and asked him to sit down and have some coffee. "I'll see Harry and let him know that you're here."

Bill looked towards the back of the restaurant and noticed Harry talking to Condo. Bill walked back to Harry. When Harry saw Bill walking towards him, he rose and started walking towards Bill.

"Is he the guy with the winning ticket?" Harry asked.

"Yes," Bill answered.

"Okay," said Harry. "Call him back here."

Jim was watching this transaction from his table, and he was prepared to meet Condo, but his heart was beating rapidly.

Bill introduced Jim to Harry and then Harry brought Jim back to Condo's table. "Sonny, I'd like you to meet Jim. Jim has a question he'd like to ask you."

Condo extended his hand. "It's very nice to meet you. Sit down, Jim, and have some lunch."

When Jim agreed to coffee and pie, Condo signaled the waiter to their table. When the waiter took the order, he left and returned quickly with the pie and coffee. Bill excused himself, saying he had to return to work.

Jim was now alone with Condo. "So, what is it that you think I may be interested in?" Condo asked.

"I'm sure you heard that I have a winning lotto ticket that's good for four million dollars."

"Yeah, I heard you hit. Congratulations."

Jim thanked him and got right down to business. "How would you like to buy the ticket for cash?" He then blurted out the bank loan story and the fact that the banks had no interest. "Now, the question is, are you interested?"

"Yes, I am." Sonny answered. "Do you have the ticket with you?"

"No," answered Jim, "but I do have it in a very safe place."

"I hope so," Sonny said. "The ticket is worth $4,000,000, right?" Jim nodded. "When did you hit?"

"About six weeks ago."

"I understand that a winner has a year to claim the money," Sonny said.

"That's right," Jim said.

"How much is taken right off the top by the state and government?"

"About twenty percent, I think," Jim said.

"Twenty percent off four million leaves what?" They sat to figure it out. "That leaves $3,200,000. Now," Condo said, "how much a month or year will that pay the winner?"

"I figure $160,000 once a year for twenty years," answered Jim.

"What's wrong with that? Why not just hold the ticket and get the money each year for twenty years?"

"Nothing is wrong with that at all, except that if I can get the money up front, there's a lot more that I can do with it."

"Such as?"

"Buy a house for cash, a new car, travel, pay for my grandchildren's' education. The whole bit," Jim explained.

By this time, Jim had finished the pie and coffee and the waiter had cleared the table. While Jim was talking to Condo, he noticed quite a few guys come into the restaurant and look over towards Sonny, trying to get his eye to talk to him. *I guess these guys are asking each other "Who is this guy with Sonny?"* Jim thought.

Sonny seemed very interested and leaned over to Jim. "Just how much money would you want for the ticket? And another thing, did you sign the back of the ticket? There's nobody's name on it, right?"

"There's no name on it," he assured Sonny. "I figure that the ticket is worth two and a half million."

Sonny looked straight ahead. "That's a lot of dough. You do understand that, don't you?"

"Yes, of course I understand," Jim said.

"If I can come up with that kind of dough, just where would you keep it? What do you have on your mind? I'd like to know."

"If the deal goes okay," Jim began, "and you buy the ticket, then I'll spread the money around my whole family, buy a house, car, clothes and such, and then put five to ten thousand in as many CDs in banks as much as possible."

Sonny said, "Yeah, because you know that you could never let such an amount of dough like that just lay around for more reasons than one."

Jim agreed. "I wonder what two and a half million looks like in one place? You know that there should be no bill over a hundred dollar bill because if there was ever a load of larger bills, there may be a lot of Feds or other law guys who may come and ask a lot of questions."

"Yes, you're right," Sonny said. "Give me your number, and if I can see how this thing can be handled, then I will call you."

"I'll tell you what, Sonny. I don't want you to call me right now. Why don't we just leave this go for a few days and I'll drop down to see you again in about a week."

"Okay," Sonny agreed. "I'll think it over and give you a better answer. So do that, drop down sometime next week and I'll let you know what can be done."

It was almost three o'clock. Jim walked out of the restaurant. On his way out, he noticed some guys looking him over as he left. Jim was feeling very nervous.

After the subway ride back uptown; and, as he walked home from the station, a million things were turning around in Jim's head. Then Jim started to wonder if he was being followed. He was feeling a little uneasy and stopped to look back. He walked back the same way he'd just come, checking to see if he was being followed. He wouldn't put anything past these guys who he figured would do anything for a buck. After making a lot of turns and walking from one side of the street to the other and back again, Jim finally got home.

"How did it go?" Mae asked.

"I think so far, so good. On the way home, I started to get a little uneasy. I wouldn't put anything past these guys to bust right in the door with guns drawn and force us to hand over the ticket."

"I told you how careful you have to be," Mae said. "I wouldn't trust them for one minute."

"Yeah, I know."

Chapter 9

The next few days were slow-paced. Bill went back into the restaurant for lunch on Tuesday of the next week. Chinatown Harry came over to him and told him to tell his friend that Sonny wanted to talk to him on Thursday at one. Bill called Jim to relay the message. Jim said he'd be there.

On Thursday, Jim rose early in the morning. He was feeling pretty good and thought that Condo would say that they could make the deal. Taking the subway back downtown, it was just a short time until Jim got to the restaurant. As he entered, he met Bill leaving to go back to work. Jim stood inside the doorway and looked over to where Condo was sitting. As usual, Condo was talking to two guys.

Harry came over to Jim. "Take it easy for a few minutes," Harry told Jim. "Sit down and have a cup of coffee. Sonny will be right with you."

A few minutes later, the guys who were talking to Condo left. Jim walked over to Condo's table.

"Hello, Jim. Sit down. Over the past week, I tried to put a lot of angles together. I think that the only way I can put that kind of money together is to bring in some other people."

"Well," Jim said, "I really don't care who or where the money comes from except for one thing. I will only talk to you. I don't want to meet or see anybody else. If the time comes when you have the money, then you and I will close the deal."

"Yeah, all right," Sonny said. "I understand what you mean. Jim, now here is what I've done. I did talk to a few people and they said that they might be able to help. I just want you to know that we are moving on this matter and maybe in a few more days we'll be able to settle this."

"That sounds good, so I'll drop down again in a few days. Or should we say the same time again here on next Thursday?"

"Yes," said Condo, "I think that would be okay."

Again, Jim left the restaurant glancing back once in a while over his shoulder just to see if he was being followed. Jim thought to himself, *I guess they won't try anything right now.* It wouldn't be too hard for a few hoods to snatch the ticket off he and Mae by coming to the house and forcing them to give up the ticket. He wondered if he finally got the money off Condo, would Condo have a couple of guys just stick a gun in their backs and take the money off them. One way or another, Jim had to be more than careful. On the subway and finally nearing home, these kinds of thoughts kept going through his head.

Jim told Mae about his meeting with Condo and what was said. She was preparing their dinner and, as usual, started to feel very uneasy. "Jim, I think that you better handle this thing without telling me any more about whatever is going on, because the more you tell me, the more I am getting worried. I keep telling you that I think you should forget this whole business with Condo and just turn the ticket into the state and be thankful that you were so lucky to hit the lotto like you did."

"I know that you are right, Mae. I may wind up kicking myself in the ass for not listening to you, but as I told you or tried to explain, this is the one way we can do all the things that we want and still have a load of dough to put into investments, checking and savings accounts. As a matter of fact, we may even make a lot more money on it than we think just from the interest from all these CDs and savings."

"Yes," Mae said, "but I am starting to get very worried about you and this whole thing. If you continue to see and meet with Condo, you better do it on your own and just don't tell me about it anymore. I am getting too nervous and I certainly don't want you to get beaten up and robbed or shot or anything like that. Just don't tell me any more."

"Okay, I'll try my best not to worry you about this any more."

"Jim, do you think for one minute that you are going to just walk in here after you settle with those people with $2,500,000 and they're going to let you just walk out of that restaurant like that with all of that money?"

"Of course not," Jim said. "I think when the time comes, it will not be in that restaurant where the money would be passed. I'm sure that they will set up a place where the money will be put up and I will turn over the ticket."

"Where would this place be?" Mae asked. "Do you think you can trust them and just give them the winning ticket and they'll hand over all of that money and you walk out of wherever this place is?"

"I would not be surprised if the place to turn over the ticket and get the money is not even in New York City. I think that it's possible that it could be down on Long Island or up in Connecticut, or even New Jersey. Who knows where and how these guys operate?"

"That's what I'm talking about."

"I don't blame you," Jim told her. "When the time comes for the payoff, here's what I think I will do. First of all, I know that I will need somebody with me just to make sure that I'll be safe and nothing should go wrong. So I was thinking I will ask Chick Thompson, Butch Dunlevy, Jim the Gin and Mike Vilk to come with me. I figure I will tell them as little as possible. I'll tell them that it's just a business deal and that I will give them each five hundred dollars for being with me. Maybe I'll ask Larry Whalen to come along too, and besides them, I think I'll try to get someone who works in a bank who can recognize funny money when they see it. You know, you can never put anything past these guys. They may even try to use a few cartons that have a few rows of money on top of each carton and underneath the money, just stacks of cut-up newspaper. What I'm getting at is, each load of money has to be counted and looked over to make sure that it's all good and not phony."

"What do you think Chick Thompson and the rest of the guys are going to say when they see all this money? I think that you'll have to tell them what this is all about."

"I'll just leave it alone until I meet Condo again and see what he can come up with. You know, it's very possible that Condo may not want to go through with the deal and just call everything off."

"I hope Condo does call it off," Mae said.

The week passed and Bill, as usual, was having his lunch at the restaurant when Chinatown Harry came over to him and told him that Condo said Jim should drop down to the restaurant for a talk.

The next day, Thursday, Jim walked into the restaurant at 1 P.M. and went right over to Condo. Sonny welcomed him and suggested that he have some coffee.

"Jim," Sonny began, "most likely I'll have to bring in some other people. It's simply too much money to raise alone."

"That's okay with me," Jim said.

"Look, don't interrupt me. I just want to give you this as straight as I can. My friends want to know how would it be for them to put up one-half now and the other half about a year from now. That way, they can have a better chance to raise the money."

Jim cut in, "No good! I'm not interested in any deal such as that."

"You don't have anything to worry about. I'll guarantee the dough and all the protection that you'll need—just in case any other problem should turn up," Sonny added.

"The money will have to be put up, all of it, the first time we meet," Jim said.

"You're driving a hard bargain."

"Your name is going on the ticket, right?"

"Maybe," Condo said. "It may be worked that way. I'm not sure."

"Why not? How can anyone else's name go on it? It could always show that you have a good income if you are ever asked where you make a living."

Condo got a little ruffled at this comment. "Jim, I think I told you before, don't lose any sleep over me being asked where I make a living. I told you before that that's my business, and furthermore, I am not too sure that you're not getting more out of this bargain than I am. As a matter of fact, I may be getting the short end of the stick all the way. It may cost me more dough than it's worth."

"No matter how you slice it," Jim said, "you will be making about $700,000 on the deal over a twenty year period."

"But," said Condo, "that's just the thing we don't like. It's tough to lay out such a big load of dough and then have to wait twenty years to get it back."

"You're not just getting it back. You are making $700,000 on the deal and that's a lot of money, even if you wait twenty years to get it back. Don't think," Jim added, "that I didn't think of a lot of other people who are millionaires who just may be very interested in a deal like this. They may get a kick out of seeing their pictures in the paper and on television as a lotto winner, and that even goes for you. As far as I go, I would just as soon flag all that glamour for one big reason. That is what nobody knows about me certainly can't hurt me. I'd rather stay out of the limelight."

Condo was annoyed. "What the hell do you think? Do you think that I like the limelight?"

"Yes. I do. I think that you get a kick out of all the attention you get."

"Well, there are times that I don't mind, but there are times that if I ever get my hands on some of these reporters, I could make it very unpleasant for them and not feel one bit sorry about it."

"What do you want to do, set up another date for a talk, or just forget the whole thing?"

"No, no," said Condo, "I'll keep in touch with you and as soon as I can, I'll tell you if it's a deal or not." Jim said he was leaving for home. "Okay," Sonny said, "I'll be in touch."

A few days later, Jim said to Mae, "You know, it's about two months since I hit that lotto and it's funny, I never see anything in the papers about how the winning ticket was never claimed."

"Maybe there are a lot of other tickets that were never claimed either," Mae said.

"Yes, but a winner only has a year to claim the money. Wouldn't you think that the papers would say how many tickets were never claimed at all?"

"I'll be glad when this is all settled," Mae said. "I hope that Condo tells you they are not interested and to just forget the whole thing."

"Yes, I agree," Jim said, then added, "if Condo doesn't come up with the money soon, I'll turn the ticket into the state. By the way, Mae, did you check under the rug to see if the ticket is still there?"

"Yes. I was cleaning the closet out the other day and looked to make sure. It's there."

"I'm going to look to make sure. It would be hot stuff if we never knew it was missing," Jim said.

"After all of this, that's all that would have to happen," Mae said as Jim left to check the ticket. It was still there.

"You know what else I've been thinking?"

"Now what?" she asked.

He laughed. "I was wondering about all of these previous lotto winners, especially the big ones."

"Why?"

"Well, you figure after they bought a house, a car and all of the other things that we said we'd like to do, how many or all of the winners must still play the lotto. I wonder how much per week that they play. I never heard of them hitting twice or more. I guess they could hit the four numbers, or even five numbers, but I never heard of them hitting the lotto for a big one again. I read about a young guy who works down on Wall Street. He says he plays about two hundred a week. He says he hit the four numbers quite often and he hit the five numbers often, but never the big one."

Jim and Mae got a call from their daughter, inviting them over for Sunday dinner. She told them that most of the family was going to be there and told them to come over early. On Sunday, Jim and Bill were sitting in the living room, watching football. They said little as they watched the game, ate cheese and crackers and drank beer, waiting for the rest of the family to arrive.

All the kids were happy to see each other. They started to run and play right away. The women were all in the kitchen and the men were together with Jim watching television. Jim knew that the only one he told about the lotto ticket was Bill. Not even Bill's wife knew about the ticket because Jim told him not to tell anyone. He was never too sure that Bill did not tell his wife.

Jim said to Bill, "You know what I've been thinking?" At this his other sons-in-law did not pay any attention. "I was thinking of switching the ticket on Condo and just giving him an old ticket and tell him that it's the winner."

Bill said, "Now I know you are nuts. What the hell kind of a nut are you, anyway?"

Jim started to laugh, then was almost doubled over with laughter.

Bill said, "I don't see anything funny in this. Not only will you get yourself killed but me also."

The other sons-in-law stopped looking at the game and started to ask what was going on, and even the women came in from the kitchen asking what happened. "What's so funny?"

"Your old man is going nuts," Bill said. "Jim, I think that you better tell the rest of the family what this is all about because sooner or later, they will know anyway."

Everybody was getting all excited. Mae stood there in silence. One by one they turned to her. "What is it, Mom? What happened?"

She shrugged her shoulders. "You should ask your father. I don't have anything to say about it."

"Ask him what?" they asked.

"Yes," Jim said. "I guess this would be as good a time to tell all of you about our good luck. I don't want any of the grandchildren to hear this. Tell them all to go out to play."

When the kids were outside, Jim settled down and told them that he had won the lotto. He told them how he tried to get a loan or sell the ticket to a bank and get as much money up front as possible. He explained that the banks were not interested in his plan. He told them he couldn't think of anyone until Bill mentioned seeing Sonny Condo in a restaurant downtown. He explained that Condo is there at the same restaurant every day and always sits at the last table in the back.

Susan, his youngest daughter, broke in, "Don't tell us that you want anything to do with this Sonny Condo?"

Jim answered, "Yes, here's what I did. As a matter of fact, the deal is practically set."

"Like what?" she asked.

"Well, when Bill told me about seeing Condo, I asked him, after thinking about it for sometime, to see if he could talk to Condo and ask him if he'd be interested in a deal to buy the lotto ticket off me. So Bill asked a guy who's always around Condo, named Chinatown Harry. Harry asked Condo and Condo said yes. A meeting was set up for me to go down and talk to him. I want to tell all of you that we never were trying to hide anything, especially not from all of you. It was just to keep quiet for the time being."

"Well, Dad," Susan asked, "when did you hit the lotto?"

"About two months ago," he answered, "and I have to tell you, I have about ten months left to turn the ticket in, one way or the other."

"What are you trying to prove?" she asked.

"Not much, except that if I can get as much money up front as possible, I can get away without paying taxes, plus have all the cash and do whatever I want."

"I think that you're crazy. How could you ever get such ideas in your head? To think that people like Condo would just hand over a lot of cash to you and just let you walk away is being very foolish. Furthermore, just how much money would you expect Condo to give you for this ticket?"

"$2,500,000."

The family was absolutely shocked. They all started talking at once, asking all kinds of questions. They were all sure that the old man had lost his mind.

"All right," Jim said. "Let's quiet down and try to listen to reason."

By this time, the football game was over and no one even knew who had won the game. No one was paying attention to the food cooking in the kitchen or to the children.

"Well," Jim said. "I've been meeting with Condo for about a month and laid out a lot of groundwork to give him the winning ticket for the $2,500,000. Condo did say it was a bit of a problem to come up with that much money in cash in one shot. He asked if the money could be settled half the first year and the rest the second year. I told him it was no good. The money had to be one time, all cash, nothing larger than one hundred dollar bills. At our last meeting, Condo told me to give him some more time and he'd let me know if he could handle it. So that's where it stands."

One of his daughters asked, "Well, what is this other matter all about? You want to switch the ticket?"

"I was just kidding. I know I could never get away with a thing like that. It was just a thought that popped into my head and I thought that it would be real funny. You know, Condo could never run to the police or anything like that."

They all started to yell at once. "Yes, but you know what would happen to you and maybe even to the rest of the family because they would want their money back."

"Yes," he said. "I know that they are a bunch of sore losers."

"That's not so funny," someone said. "What are you going to do now? And just what would you do with so much cash around the house at one time?"

Jim said. "I'm going to get four or five guys to be with me when I pass the ticket to Condo and get the cash. I want to get a guy who maybe works in a bank who would know phony money when he saw it."

One son-in-law said, "They'll never pay off in phony money because if you were ever caught using it, they wouldn't want it traced back to them."

"I figure I would give each one of the guys $1,000 each for their trouble. Then, we would go some place where we'll be safe so we can look over the money and put it in a safe place."

"Where will that be?" Ed asked.

"Well, that's a bit of a problem. I think that we should use two cars to go to Condo's place to close the deal. When we leave, we use two bags to carry the money—one in one car, and the other in the second car. I think I'll have to have one of you guys with me in the second car to watch that bag of money. Then we should go to my house where all of you should be waiting for me. After paying off the guys, I will give each of you a bag of cash that you'll each have to hold onto and take care of. Nobody is to go out and start to blow the money on a lot of foolish nonsense and just have a good time. I will want to meet and set up arrangements to invest the money. I also want you all to put the money in small bank accounts and CDs and we'll have to do this each day in order to cut down on having so much cash around the house. If any of us needs a new car, house, or anything, we'll take care of it just as soon as possible. That's just about where things stand right now," Jim concluded. "So, let's have supper. If anyone has any suggestions to make, let's hear them."

With that, Jim's youngest son-in-law, Dave, spoke up. "I know a guy very well who works in a bank. He's an assistant manager who should know bad money when he sees it."

"Who is he?"

"His name is Marty Carroll. I think you met him at our house a few times."

"Yeah," Jim said, "I remember him. Yes. I think he would be a good guy to have with us."

After dinner, they all felt pretty good, but still were trying to settle down with thoughts of becoming millionaires. It still had them all excited and they talked about the things they'd like to do and the places they'd like to go. Before long, the grandchildren were getting tired and restless and wanted to go home.

Mae said, "I think we'd better leave and all of us go home and try to get a good night's sleep."

Dolly and her husband, Ed, said that it was a very frightening thing to have so much cash in the house. "Just suppose," said Dolly, "we're all followed home to our houses, or even just one of us and someone breaks in or comes in with a gun and holds us up."

Jim answered, "Listen, I want to be as careful as I can. That's the reason I want to have a few guys with us just to let Condo know that we are not alone. These guys, all of them, have been up against many a tough hood, and these guys don't scare so easily. When the time comes to give up the ticket and get the money, I'm pretty sure that we will be in and out of the place pretty fast. It's getting late," Jim said, checking his watch. "It's about time we hit the road. We have to get the subway back to Manhattan."

Chapter

As Jim and Mae walked towards the subway, they reflected on their family, as they often did. They were so lucky to have such wonderful daughters, sons-in-law and grandchildren. Nancy, their middle daughter, had married Bill. They lived in Elmhurst, Queens in a nice apartment. Their three children all attended the local grade school. Bill worked for a coffee broker downtown and had an office job.

Dolly, their oldest daughter, and her husband, Ed, had two teenage daughters in high school. Ed was a checker on the docks in Brooklyn. Their youngest daughter, Susan, and her husband, Dave, lived in the Bronx near Gunn Hill Road, not far from where Dave pulls out. Dave is a tractor-trailer driver for one of the big food chain supermarkets. He had a very good union job.

When Jim and Mae got home to their old seven room flat on the west side, it was close to 11 P.M. and they were both tired. It had been a long and exciting day.

As they prepared for bed, Jim said, "It really was hot stuff the way all the kids got so excited after hearing about us winning the lotto."

"What did you expect them to do? Sure they were excited. Who wouldn't be? For that matter, you seem to be taking this whole business as some kind of a big joke."

"No. I don't think so," Jim said. "I'm trying to be as careful as I can be."

Mae repeated what she had said so often over the past few weeks. "I wish you would just forget the whole thing and turn in the winning ticket to the lotto. We'll be just as well off. Who knows what may happen? Even if we do get all of this money, who's to say that all our troubles will be over."

"Listen," Jim said, "we've gone this far, so let's not get worried or even think about things not going all right for all of us. You know how many times that I told you and the kids that this is only the second flat I ever lived in? I was born and raised next door and when we got married, we took this flat and it's as far as I got ever since I retired from the waterfront."

"Yes." Mae said, "I've heard that story a thousand times, and I still say we should just turn the ticket into the lotto."

"Yes, I know, but like I said before, I remember when these rooms had no heat, only hot water, and we had gas for cooking and light. We used to use a gas mantle to spread the light in the kitchen and dining rooms. The others just had a gas pipe coming out of the wall. The biggest improvements that I've seen in my life are steam heat and electricity. We don't even own a car, so that is the reason I want to try and get all this money all at once. Then we can do a load of things, especially with the kids and their families. You know, you have to hand it to the girls. After all, they are good wives and mothers, taking care of their homes and their kids, cooking, cleaning and all that work every day. They never seem to go any place or do any complaining. They are really good daughters and we should be very proud of them."

"Yes. I know," said Mae, "but I am very tired after this day, so let's just go to bed and get some rest."

Chapter

The week passed uneventfully until Friday afternoon. Jim got a phone call from Bill who had a message from Condo. Bill, as usual, was having lunch at the same restaurant. Harry had come over to him and told him to tell Jim that Sonny wanted to talk to him on Monday at 1 P.M.

"That's good, Bill. I'll be down there on Monday. If I get there a little early, I may see you before you go back to work. But if I don't see you, I will keep in touch," Jim said.

That weekend, Jim said to Mae, "Do you notice that Condo never said to have the winning ticket with me? He didn't make any reference at all, so I'll just take it easy until I talk to him and see what he has to say."

Jim barely slept over the weekend. After he got ready for his Monday meeting, he kissed Mae. "Leave a light in the window for me, okay?"

Exiting the downtown subway, Jim walked the few blocks to the restaurant. He looked over to where Bill usually sat at the counter, but Bill wasn't there. Jim looked toward the rear and saw Condo. Condo noticed him right away and waved for Jim to come back to the table. Condo was alone. Some guys were sitting at a table nearby, but they just seemed to be talking among themselves. Chinatown Harry was not around.

"Hello, Sonny, how are you?"

"Okay. Sit down." When Jim was seated, Sonny asked. "So, how do you feel?"

"I feel great. Things couldn't be better."

"Okay, let's get down to business. Jim, by any chance, do you have the ticket on you?"

"No."

"Yes, of course," Condo said. "That is best. Keep it in a safe place until we close the deal, if we can."

"That's what I'm here for. Do you want to set up a date, time and place, or would you want to meet me some place?"

"The thing," Sonny said, "is the money. Do you realize what a big amount of dough that this is? You are talking about $2,500,000 cash right up front."

"Yes, that's what I'm talking about, and that's the way it will have to be."

"All right now," Condo said, "where I get the money from or if anybody else is in on this with me is none of your business, of course."

"I could care less," Jim said.

"I have to tell you that I do have to talk to a few friends and bring them in on it with me."

"That's your business," Jim said.

"Okay, I know it is. You know, I'm still not sure that I'm not getting the short end of the stick."

"Don't forget," Jim reminded Condo, "you're getting twenty percent over twenty years. What's so bad about that? As a matter of fact, it's more than a bank would be giving. Furthermore, you know how you that can use this as a reference where you're getting income from."

Condo got a little mad about that crack. "I told you once before, don't you or anyone else ever do any worrying about how I have to show where I get my income from. I told you that is my business."

"I know," said Jim, "I was just trying to point out a hedge that you can always use. So the question is, Sonny, can you come up with the money and, if so, when can we settle this business and get it over with once and for all?"

"I usually take my time whenever I get any kind of proposition, I don't rush into anything."

"You know," said Jim, "I've talked to you about this matter on four or five occasions, including today, so I'm sure that you know where you are going and what you want to do. So if you want to make a time and place that we can meet, the sooner the better. To tell you the truth, my wife would just as soon that I turn in the ticket and get the money from lotto and just forget the whole thing."

"Well, that brings up one other thing that I've been wanting to get straight with you. Don't ever, I mean ever, in any way, shape or form, tell anybody that you ever made a deal with me. If your wife and your son-in-law know about it, make sure that no one else does," Sonny warned.

"Don't worry, no one else will know about it. You know, I would never want anybody to know that I have any money. Every freeloader in creation would be looking for me to ask for money."

Condo said, "You clearly understand, I will not do any worrying. If I ever hear that my name was mentioned, wherever you are concerned, I am telling you right now, you will be a pretty sorry man."

"I know what you mean. I don't have any intention of ever saying anything to anyone. I want to keep this as quiet as you do."

"How many kids do you have?" Condo asked.

"Three," said Jim.

"Grandchildren?"

"Yes," Jim answered, "eight."

"That sounds like a nice family," Condo said. "One other thing. Is there anyone in your family who knows me? I mean like on a business basis?"

"No, no one."

"Okay, that's good."

"I understand what you mean," Jim said.

Condo told Jim that he was thinking of meeting at a mutual place and wanted to know just how Jim was going to carry all of the money home once the transaction was complete.

"Here's what I'm going to do," Jim began. "When the time comes, and I hope that it's soon, I will meet you any place, at any time. I have to tell you that I will have a few friends with me, and I do have a guy who will look over the money and make sure that it is all good."

"Who are these friends of yours? Just what are you telling them?" Condo's eyes turned hard. "I just told you, and even asked you, was you or anybody in your family 'connected,' and you said no."

"Yes, that's right," Jim said.

Condo was annoyed. "Well, who are these guys that you want to bring with you?"

"They're just a few friends that I've known for years."

"Did any of them ever do any time?"

"Some have. But none of them are wanted by the cops. But I do have to tell you. They're some of the toughest guys in the neighborhood."

Chapter 12

"Look," Condo said, exasperated, "I'm trying to go along with you the best I can. I am not even that sure that I like this deal and we're telling each other how we have to keep this whole thing so quiet. But in the meantime, you got a couple of guys lined up to come with you when we close the deal. You even want to bring in a guy to look over the money. Did it ever occur to you that this is the last thing in the world that I would ever be interested in is phony money? Do you realize that if I paid you off in bad money and you got picked up, I know that the first thing you would do is tell the cops where you got that money from. Look," Sonny said, "if you think that you need somebody with you, and I am sure that you should have some protection, I'll tell you what I'll do. I'll have a few guys escort you to wherever you want to go with the money."

"I would appreciate that," Jim said, "but would they know what I would be carrying? I figure I would probably need a few large bags to carry the money in."

"One large suitcase will be enough because all the money will be in one hundred dollar bills. There will be stacks of hundred's, amounting to five thousand in each stack. That'll be a wrapper of five thousand in each bundle and twenty wrappers of five thousand. That means twenty-five stacks of $100,000 each comes to $2,500,000. One large suitcase should do it," Sonny said.

"Okay," Jim said. "Then all we have to know is where will we make the transfer of the ticket for the money."

Sonny said, "I have a few loose ends to cover and think that we should close the deal in a week or ten days. Today is Monday, maybe by next Wednesday or Friday at the latest. You may get a call that the whole deal is off, so don't be too upset."

"I understand," Jim told him, "because like anything, you can never tell how things will turn out. I'll just turn the ticket into the lotto people. Is there a number where I can reach you, or will you be in touch with me? The reason I say this is just so we can line up a place to close the deal. I'm thinking that we cannot very well walk into a place like this or some club and be seen with a large bag leaving. If anyone notices, maybe too many questions will be asked."

"Yes," Sonny said. "I know what you mean. Give me your home phone number and I'll give you a call from an outside pay phone when I'm ready." Jim wrote his home phone number on a piece of paper, but he was reluctant to do so.

"Thanks," said Sonny.

"I'll wait until I hear from you," Jim said.

• • •

On the subway back uptown, Jim started to worry about that phone number being found on Condo. Suppose Condo got picked up for anything and the cops asked him whose phone number it was. Of course, they could easily find out who had that number. Jim thought that when he did finalize this deal with Condo, he'd tell him to tear up that phone number. He could always get the phone company to change the number and keep an unlisted number in the future.

After finally reaching his apartment, Jim walked up the four flights of stairs to his apartment. On the way up, he got an idea about meeting in some place out of the way when the transfer took place. He thought that a motel some place would be best for the deal.

Mae met Jim at the door, as usual, and was quite excited. "Is everything all right?" she asked him.

Jim assured her that everything was fine. "Is there anything the matter here? You sound upset."

"No, I'm fine. It's just that the idea of you going downtown to meet these people and getting home that keeps me worried. I can't wait until this is all settled. Then I can breathe easily again."

"Everything went well," Jim assured her.

"Good."

"Condo said that he thinks he'll be ready to close the deal in maybe a week to ten days. We will set up a date and a place to finish our business. Sonny said that I do not have to bring any people in to count the money or examine it. It will be in stacks of one hundred dollar bills, $5,000 in each stack. He said that if I felt like I need anybody with me, that he'd get a few guys to escort us any place we want to go. He reminded me that I'm the one who wanted to keep this as quiet as possible. You know, Mae, he makes a lot of sense. I get the impression that I can trust him."

"Are you kidding? I wouldn't trust him as far as I could throw him."

"Yes. I know, Mae."

● ● ●

After dinner, they watched the news on television in silence. Jim was thinking, as usual, of every angle that he could. *Just how will the deal be closed? When and where? Who should know? Who can be trusted to be with me when the deal is finally made?*

Jim thought that one of the kids would call, but there were no phone calls that night. During the next few days, Mae spoke to the kids and some friends a few times on the phone. No one besides Mae, Jim, their daughters and sons-in-law knew anything about the lotto ticket. When the kids called, they were smart enough to not ask any questions over the phone. At the end of the week, Dave called Jim.

"I'm surprised I haven't heard from anybody before now," Jim said.

"Well, I was thinking of a place for you to use if you think it could be any good," Dave suggested.

"That's great! Where is it?"

"I'll tell you, but maybe we better come down to your house."

"How about you, Susan and the kids come down for Sunday dinner tomorrow? You can let me know what you have on your mind," Jim said.

"Okay," Dave said. "We'll come down about 3 P.M."

On Sunday at 3 P.M., Dave, Susan and the kids drove down to the west side. Jim was anxious to see them not only because Dave may have an idea for him, but also because Jim and Mae always got such a kick out of seeing the grandchildren.

When the family was settled, Dave and Jim went into the living room to talk.

"What were you thinking about?" Jim asked.

"Well, this is the way I understand the picture. First of all, you say that you are thinking of asking a few close friends to go with you when you collect the money from Condo. Well," Dave said, "I'm not so sure that's a good idea. You told us at Nancy's house last week that above all, nobody is to know about you winning the lotto. How are you going to keep it quiet if these guys you mentioned know about you winning and settling for all that money? I was wondering if maybe you and Condo could meet someplace out of the way, where nobody would recognize any particular person coming or going."

"Where?" Jim asked.

"At a hotel or motel. Have these people who are going to bring the money meet you there. Then you turn over the ticket to them."

"That sounds like a good idea," Jim said. "Condo told me it was not necessary to have anyone checking the money to see if it was counterfeit. He told me that if I need a few guys to protect us, to make sure no one tries a fast one on us, that he would send a couple of guys over to make sure that nothing happens."

"That sounds pretty good, but how do you know that these very same guys don't just put a bullet into you after you give them the winning ticket and just take the money, ticket and all? Who says you can trust them?" Dave asked.

"I know that this may sound foolish, but I sort of do trust Condo. He seems like a nice guy."

"Yeah," Dave said, "I know, but all these guys are nice until you really know them. And if they took the money off you after you gave them the ticket, what are you going to do about it? You can't run to the cops, either."

"You sure are right there," said Jim. "I was being funny when I said that if I could pull a switch on Condo by giving him a ticket that was not a winner, what could he do about it, certainly not sue me. We know that my life would not be worth a plug nickel and that they would certainly make sure they got their money back. I have to say that you have given me a good idea, Dave. Maybe that will be the best way to set up the deal. As I think about your ideas, you can think about a hotel where we can meet where there will be a lot of people around so these guys, or anyone else, would not want to try any tricks. Let me think about this.

"I went down to see Condo a few days ago and at that time, he said it would be a week or ten days before he could put up all that dough. I guess he's bringing a few people in it with him, but that's his business. I can just imagine him coming forward with the ticket as a lotto winner. He's a real ham and loves the attention that he gets."

"You do have the ticket in a safe place, don't you?" Dave asked.

"Yes, of course," Jim said.

"Did Condo ever ask you to let him see the ticket to make sure that you did hit the lotto? Because most likely, you will have to show him how the winning numbers appeared in the newspapers."

"Condo did ask me once if I had the ticket with me and I told him no, but that it was in a safe place and that I did not sign it. I told him that when he has the money, I will give it to him. It will be hot stuff when he claims the money. This is one picture that I want to see. Then the reporters will be asking him why he waited so long to claim the money."

"When did you hit it anyway?" Dave asked.

"September."

"Well, this is November. That's about two months," Dave said.

Jim nodded. "It should be a great Christmas for the whole family."

"That's one thing I'm looking forward to. It will be the greatest Christmas ever for all of us."

Jim paused for a few moments, deep in thought. "Dave, your idea of using a hotel to close the deal is a very good one. I wonder just what hotel to use. I suppose we will have to make reservations."

"That'll be no problem," Dave assured him. "So just as soon as you know when Condo is ready with the money, the reservations can be made." Dave and Jim were silent with their own thoughts for a moment.

"How about the Story Hotel on 7th Avenue?" Dave brightened. "That should be a good place. There's always lots of people coming and going and I think that no one there would pay any attention to whoever we are or who we're meeting."

"You're giving me a lot to think about, Dave," Jim said. "That may be the best way to set this up. Maybe what we ought to do is have one of us call the hotel in advance and reserve a room. Maybe Susan can do that from your house in the Bronx. Maybe we should reserve three rooms right next to each other."

"Why three?" Dave asked.

"We should reserve three rooms right next to each other. You and Susan can take one room, Bill and Nancy can take the other and Mae and I will take the middle room. With the rooms connected to each other, we can keep in touch and have our bags with us to carry the money out without anybody being suspicious of us. Yes," Jim said, "I think that would be a good idea. As soon as I hear from Condo, I'll tell him that's where we will close the deal."

"You'll have to think of one other thing," Dave said.

"What's that?" Jim asked.

"You will have to have the winning ticket on you, right?" Jim nodded in agreement. "How would it be to make some other arrangements?"

"Like what?"

"I don't know just yet. Do you think that you can just hand over the ticket to these people? I think you better be more careful than that."

"Yes, yes," Jim said. "The more we talk about this, the more we need to do something. I do think that the hotel idea is a good one, but maybe we better think a little more about it. If you get any other thoughts on this, give me a call. In the meantime, I will talk to Bill and Ed and tell them what we've been talking about and see if they have any ideas."

Mae and Susan called them to come and eat. After dinner, when the table was cleared and Mae and Susan were washing the dishes, Jim and Dave still sat at the table.

"Dave, after you leave, I will give Bill and Ed a call and then we'll just take it easy for a few days and see if Sonny is ready with the money."

Dave, Susan and the kids left for home around 9 P.M. Shortly after, Jim called Ed, then Bill. He related to both of them the conversation that he had with Dave. Jim warned Bill that Condo might contact him first when he's ready to close the deal.

"I don't think so," Bill told Jim. "As of now, Condo most likely doesn't want anyone else in on it. I think that Condo will contact you."

"Well, maybe he'll work it that way," Jim answered. "Bill, I just want you to know everything that's happening."

Chapter 13

Jim said to Mae, "Before we go to sleep, I'd like to tell you a few things about this Sonny Condo and his mob."

"Like what?" Mae asked.

"Well, like the guys who associate with or work for Condo. It seems that no matter how loyal they are to him, they all seem to have a racket of their own besides whatever they make with Condo, such as shake downs or loan sharking."

"How do you know about these things?" Mae asked.

"Well," Jim said, "It's a lot of little things. They all want to be so smart and wise that nobody should know what they are up to, but it is written all over them with the moves they make and sometimes you cannot help but hear them. Take this guy Chinatown Harry. He told Bill and some of the guys who eat with him every day how he knows a few manufacturers on Crosby Street and Mercer Street where he buys loads of work jackets for cash. He said he pays twelve dollars a jacket and sells them for fifteen dollars, making three dollars profit on each one. Harry's trick is to make all his contacts think that these jackets are swag*.

"It's the way Harry sidles up to these guys. He's always looking around and watching out for some imaginary FBI agent or a cop as he's giving a spiel to a potential buyer. Harry has to let them think that these jackets are hot swag and for these guys to keep their mouths shut. So at these points, the buyers are more than anxious to get in on a good buy. Now that Harry has their attention and confidence, he tells them that these jackets are made for the big department stores and made to sell for thirty-nine dollars each. As soon as these guys hear that, now they get all excited and want to buy three or four jackets at fifteen dollars

* stolen

each. They figure that they have sons or brothers who also can use a new jacket."

Jim went on to tell Mae, "Harry controls a few shop stewards on jobs at warehouses, trucking companies and the docks. He gets these guys to take at least two dozen jackets at a time to sell to the guys they work with. These shop stewards sell the jackets for twenty dollars each and make five dollars on each.

"Harry's also done a little money-lending on the side, of course—lending out money and making sure that he was paid back with interest. He'd always let these people, who wanted to borrow money, know how the mob was behind him and that it was actually their money he was lending out. The reason for all of this was to make sure that the borrower would be sure to pay back with big interest at the end of each week.

"Harry, like the rest of the crew who worked for Condo, would tell the borrower that he'd have to talk to the big man. This is exactly what he would do. Aside from pushing the jackets, Harry's biggest action would be as a loan shark and he could always handle this action for himself.

"When Harry went to the jacket manufacturers on Crosby and Mercer Streets, he would love to show a big wad of dough, letting those manufacturers know that he had the cash for any kind of a deal that they may want to make. The truth was, these manufacturers often out-smarted Harry. They'd tell him how business was very bad and they may have to fold up and lay off their workers.

"Then Harry would ask if they needed any money. They'd sheepishly say yes, so Harry would ask if they wanted a grand or two.

"They'd say that they could use two thousand dollars, but that they'd have to pay back in material, such as their finished jackets. Harry, wanting to be a good fellow, would say, yes. Of course, there was no mention of any interest on the loan, but Harry always thought that he had made a smart deal."

"Let's get to sleep," Mae told Jim. "I've heard enough about Chinatown Harry."

Jim started laughing. "I cannot help but tell you since I really do think that these guys are a riot." He kept talking to Mae, telling her how one day, while talking to Sonny, Harry came into the restaurant. Condo called him right over and said to him, "I'm getting a little tired of taking messages for you and these phone calls."

"So what's the difference?" Harry asked. "They're not important."

"Sounds like something is going on to me," Condo answered.

"You know that I push a few jackets once in a while. The calls are from guys who need a new jacket, that's all." Harry added, "If there was any good score being made, you know that you would be the first to know about it."

"You better make sure I know," Sonny told him.

"How about Frankie, Louie, Butchie and Teddy? Do they all keep you informed about what they are doing?" Harry said.

With that Condo said, "Harry, you'd better watch yourself. I know that all of you guys have little deals off your own, but if I keep getting annoyed with these calls and messages for all of you, I'll kick the whole damn bunch of you the hell out of here."

Chapter 14

On Tuesday evening, when the phone rang, Mae answered, and when the caller asked to speak to Jim, Mae handed him the phone. It was Condo.

After a few pleasantries, they got down to business.

"It may be an extra week or two before I have the money ready," Sonny said. "I was talking to some of my friends and one of them asked if I saw the winning ticket. I told him that I hadn't. So this guy said, 'Don't you think that you better see it before this deal goes any further?' So you'll have to show me some proof that you do have the ticket."

"Okay," Jim answered. "Suppose I have a photostat with the date of the paper, proving that it is the winner?"

"That sounds okay," Sonny said. "Get the photostat made and drop down to the lunchroom on Friday. Make sure that you have the newspaper and the ticket all photostatted together with the date of the paper showing. Then there will be no doubt that you do have the ticket. When you come down on Friday, maybe I can have a definite date when we can close the deal."

"Okay," Jim agreed. "Are you on an outside pay phone now?"

"Yes," Sonny answered. "I wouldn't call you from my home phone, so don't worry about that."

"All right," Jim said. "I'll be down to see you on Friday."

On Thursday, Jim took the ticket and the newspaper copy down to a local store that makes copies. He didn't want the man in the store to put the ticket and paper in the machine and he didn't want anyone asking questions. So, Jim tried to act like he knew just how to operate the machine. When the storeowner looked over and saw that he didn't even know how to put the paper into the machine, he approached Jim to help.

"Real quick!" Jim said. "Can you hurry? I have a very important appointment and I'm late now."

"It won't take but ten seconds," the man said.

Jim tried to keep the guy from looking and he was sure that all the guy saw was that it was a lotto ticket and newspaper together. The man didn't ask any questions. He just handed Jim the copies when the machine stopped. Jim gave him the money and beat it out of the store as fast as he could. He kept wondering if the guy in the store was smart to the winning ticket. Well, anyway, nothing could be done now. Jim headed home.

On Friday, Jim took the subway downtown and arrived at the lunchroom about one o'clock. Bill wasn't there. Jim looked towards the back of the room and saw Condo and a few guys talking to him. When Condo spotted Jim, he waved him back to his table.

"How did you make out?" he asked Jim.

"Okay. I have the photostat with me." He reached into his pocket and pulled out the copy. "Here they are."

Condo looked them over and checked the date and the numbers. "They look good."

"So, how do things look?" Jim asked. "Do you think that you are ready to set up a date for the exchange?"

"I can't tell you right now, but I will for sure sometime this coming week."

"I've been thinking about a place where we can meet," Jim said. "I think I'll get a room at the Story Hotel on 7th Avenue in advance, once we settle the date. If you give me a number to call, I'll phone you and tell you which room I'll be in. Then you or whoever you want can deliver the money and I'll turn over the ticket."

"That sounds good," Sonny agreed.

"Another thing. I don't want to be rushed. I want to count the money. I am trusting you that this better not be funny money."

"The money will be good," Sonny assured him. "Take all the time you want. When I call you again, I'll give you a number so you can let me know what room you're in."

Jim stood, shook hands with Condo and left the restaurant.

Since this was Friday and the weather was nice, Jim thought he'd walk home instead of taking the subway. Taking a casual walk always helped to clear his head and he arrived home an hour later. After entering his apartment, he told Mae about the meeting with Condo and that everything was looking pretty good.

After dinner, Jim and Mae were watching television when the phone rang. It was Condo.

"I have a much better deal for you that could go to as much as $10,000,000." Jim was hesitant and Condo reminded him that he was calling from a pay phone.

"What's the deal?" Jim asked.

"I don't want to talk to you on the phone, even this pay phone, but here's what I want you to do. If you're interested, you'll have to meet a guy who will tell you where and when this meeting will take place."

"When do you want me to meet this guy?"

"Right now," Condo said.

"Wait a minute! What's the rush? I like to take things easy and think them over before I ever make a move," Jim said.

"I don't want to mention what this deal can be, but here's what you have to do if you're interested." Jim said he was interested. "Can you get to 23rd Street and 7th Avenue by 9 P.M. tonight?"

"Yes," Jim said.

"Okay. Go there and stand at the northeast corner of 23rd Street and 7th Avenue and a guy will meet you and give you the proposition."

"Are you sure that all he's going to give me is a proposition?"

"Listen," Condo said, "all he'll do is ask you a question. If you're interested, he'll make the deal. If you're not interested, just forget it and go home. This guy will be alone, so don't have anybody with you."

"How will he know me or how will I know him?" Jim asked.

"Don't worry. The guy will just walk up to you and ask you if you're Jim. When you answer, he'll tell you what the deal is."

"Sonny," Jim said, "I don't know. I don't feel like this is a good idea. I'm not so sure that all that's going to happen is he'll ask me a question."

"Yes, that's right. Look, didn't you come to me because you wanted to make a lot of money up front instead of waiting year by year to collect from the lotto? Well," Condo said, "you had a big deal that's a lot of money. Now I have one for you, if you are interested. All you have to say is okay, and if you don't like the deal, just turn around and go home and nobody will be hurt. I really don't want to talk about this over the phone."

"That's the part I don't like," Jim said.

"If you want to make $10,000,000 instead of the $2,500,000, then be at the corner of 23rd Street and 7th Avenue at 9 P.M."

"Suppose I think it over and decide not to go?"

"That's okay. If you don't show up, the guy will not wait and nothing will be said."

"It's almost 8 P.M. now," Jim said. "If I have to be there at 9 P.M., I have to get ready. I'll have to tell Mae about this call so that if anything goes wrong, she'll have the answers in case she has to explain anything to the cops.

Condo was annoyed. "Tell her anything you want. I am telling you just once again. If you are interested, be there at 9 P.M. If you're not, don't bother. You'll get this deal from another guy, not me. I never asked you, do you understand?"

"Yes, I get it. I'll walk over there and see what it is that the guy has to say." Jim hung up and turned to Mae who was very curious about Jim's conversation.

Jim told Mae a brief version of the conversation that he'd just had with Sonny.

"I heard it," she said, "and I don't have to tell you that I don't like it."

"I'll walk over and see what this guy has to say."

"I think that you are being very foolish," Mae said sternly. "Suppose this man gets tough with you and pulls a gun or tries something else and you wind up getting hurt. What good is that going to do?"

"Yes, I know what you are saying, but as long as you keep the ticket for the lotto, at least we'll know that they're not going to get anything from us. I would like to see what this guy has to offer. So, I'll walk over to 23rd and see what he has to say."

"I wish you wouldn't," Mae said.

"I'll tell you what. Give Susan a call and tell her what I'm doing. That way, if anything happens, you can call the police and she can verify that she knew I was going to a meeting at Condo's suggestion."

Chapter 15

On his way up to 23rd Street, Jim could not help but meet some people he knew. They tried to get into a conversation with him, asking how he and Mae were, but Jim only had one thing on his mind. Jim did not want to waste any time. He also didn't want to show anyone how anxious he was about this meeting. The whole idea was that no one should know that he hit the lotto.

When he arrived at the designated spot, he stood close to the corner of the building. He felt like the whole city was watching him. As each car passed him, Jim tightened up, looked over every car, and at every person who walked passed him. At last, a nice looking car pulled up and a well dressed guy got out. He walked right over to Jim.

"Are you Jim?"

"Yes," Jim answered.

"I don't have much time," the guy said.

"Well, what's this all about?" Jim asked.

"I understand that you have a lotto ticket that you want to sell for $2,500,000 cash." Jim nodded. "Well, how would you like something for the ticket that's worth over ten million?"

"What is it?" Jim asked.

"It's dope. Heroin. All in nice clean packets. All ready for the streets."

Jim cut him off. "I am certainly not at all interested in such a deal."

"You wouldn't have any trouble pushing it on the street," the guy said. The more he kept talking, the more Jim kept moving away. Jim repeated over and over that he was not interested.

The guy finally gave up, walked to his car and drove away. Jim stood there, calling Condo all kinds of names under his breath. He wondered what kind of nut Condo was. He was supposed to be such a big shot and here he is, trying to pay me off in dope. I have a notion to tell Condo to shove it and just cash the ticket into the lotto.

While Jim had been at the meeting, Mae called Susan. "I don't like this at all," Susan told her mother. "I can't help but feel that Dad is going to really get hurt and I wish that he had never gotten involved with this thing at all. I even wish he'd never hit the lotto. Before he even gets any money, just look at all the trouble he can possibly get into. When we hang up, I'm going to call Dolly and Nancy. I think we, just the three of us, better talk to each other about all of this because there are too many things that can happen. Above all, we don't want Dad to be hurt. All the money in the world would not be worth it. I think we should see how Dolly and Nancy feel about all of this. I'm sure they're just as concerned and scared as I am."

"Okay," Mae answered. "You call Dolly and Nancy. I'm going to look out the front window and wait for your Dad to come home. I hope nothing happens to him. I'm really getting nervous. I'll be shaking like a leaf until he gets back."

"Call me as soon as Dad gets home," Susan said.

Susan called Dolly and relayed the conversation that she'd just had with her mother.

"I've been so frightened since this whole thing started," Dolly admitted. "I wish Dad hadn't gotten into this whole thing."

"Okay, Dolly," Susan said. "Listen, I've got to call Nancy and tell her what's happening and then Mom is going to call me again. Oh, I hope he's all right."

"You call Nancy and I'll call you in about an hour. I'd call Mom, but she must be petrified by now. If she keeps getting all these calls, she may get sick with worry," Dolly said.

As soon as the phone rang in Nancy's house, she picked up immediately. She was glad that it was Susan calling. Before Susan had a chance to tell her about their father's meeting, Nancy asked if something had happened to him.

"Not exactly," Susan answered. She then went on to tell Nancy about the deal that Dad was looking into.

"This is nothing but trouble, fooling around with these people." Nancy said. "Everybody knows what kind of things they do and it doesn't bother them for one minute to hurt anyone who gets in their way. I don't think I'll be able to sleep all night now. That's the way it's been ever since Dad started to deal with these people. Every night when I go to bed, I keep rolling and tossing with this on my mind. I didn't want to say anything to anyone for fear of getting them worried. Now I see that we all are starting to get jumpy."

"Listen," Nancy said, "I think it would be a good idea if the three of us meet by ourselves and go over this whole situation. God forbid that it ever gets out of hand and something happens to Dad. What would Mom ever do? Who would she live with? Where would she go? What if she ever had to live on Dad's pensions? And whatever could she get from the union? Maybe she can't get anything at all."

"I don't think that anything like that can happen," Susan said.

"Well, these are the kinds of things that keep going through my head. I'll never be satisfied until Dad gets all of this nonsense over with and things get back to normal. If he is ever hurt or killed, I don't know how I could take it. I'm going to light a candle tonight. I hope nothing happens to him," Susan said. "I guess we better get off the phone so you can get Mom's call. I'll call you back in an hour or two. Dolly will be calling you, right?"

"Yes," Susan answered. "Call me in an hour or two and I'll fill you and Dolly in. We'll have to meet, maybe at some restaurant in midtown for lunch. We'll see if we can work out some kind of action just in case anything happens to Dad. We really should talk over what we should do if we ever get all of that money."

When he got home, Mae was watching out the window. When she saw Jim coming down the street, she breathed a sigh of relief. "Thank God," she said. She went to the door and opened it, waiting for Jim. "Are you all right? Did anything happen?" she asked anxiously.

"I'm okay, but I did not make any deal. What a creep!" Jim entered the apartment and told Mae about the guy's offer.

"The nerve of those people!" Mae said, indignant. "They must be into everything. It goes to show how you cannot trust them. Susan told me to call her back as soon as you got home to let her know that you're all right. Let me give her a call."

"Go ahead," Jim said, "I'm going to fix myself a drink, then we can talk some more."

When Mae got off the phone with Susan, she sat with Jim in the living room. They watched television in silence for a while.

"I'll give Condo one more week and if he doesn't come up with the money, well, the hell with him. I'll just cash it in and that will settle everything. Now I am kind of sorry I ever bothered trying to sell the ticket. I should have listened to you and not tried to be so damn smart."

"Well," Mae said, "try to take it easy and don't go getting yourself upset."

"I guess you're right," said Jim.

Chapter 16

The next day Dolly, Nancy and Susan decided to meet at Nancy's house in Queens. When they all got settled down and started to talk, Dolly said that she and Ed did go over this situation a few times. "Ed told me one night during one of these discussions how he knows a few tough guys on the pier in Brooklyn where he is a checker. Ed said that he got to know these guys pretty well and did hear how they would be making a score. Of course, Ed never got involved, but he could not help but listen since they would talk right out in front of him. Ed got an idea that maybe he could ask one of these tough guys from the docks for a gun and then he'll let Dad carry it with him when the time comes to collect the money for the lotto ticket. I told Ed that I didn't think this was such a good idea because Dad could get caught with a loaded gun. Plus, if Sonny Condo ever found out that Dad had a gun on him, he may blow his top and there might be some shooting. Dad could get hurt."

"We don't want Dad going anywhere carrying a gun no matter how much money is involved," Nancy said.

I think we should tell Dad to turn the ticket into lotto and just forget the whole thing," Susan said. "This whole thing is just getting real crazy.

"Please don't get mad at Ed," Dolly said. "He's only thinking of Dad and he wants Dad to be prepared and to protect himself."

Nancy and Susan both told Dolly they were sure that Ed had Dad's best interest in mind, but the thought of him carrying a gun was just too much.

"That idea is out," Nancy said. "If Dad wanted a gun, he could get one from one of the guys on the west side that he knows."

"Yes, I guess you're both right," Dolly said. "I did tell Ed that I didn't want Dad to get hurt or arrested."

The girls discussed some ideas about how the money should be handled if and when this whole business got settled.

"We'll all have to just wait and see how things turn out," Susan said.

After lunch, Dolly and Susan got ready to leave. They hugged and kissed each other, hoping that everything would turn out all right and that nothing would happen to their father.

"I'd like everyone to come to my house for Thanksgiving dinner," Dolly offered.

Susan and Nancy agreed that it would be great to be together.

Chapter

The weekend passed quietly as usual. Mae had gotten phone calls from the kids. She told them all about the deal that was offered and they all agreed that a deal like that, where dope was concerned, was out of the question.

On Wednesday, Condo called. He got right to the point, never mentioning anything about the deal with the guy on 23rd Street.

"Everything is okay and the money is ready," he told Jim. "You said you'd get a room up at the Story Hotel, right?" Jim told him that he would. "Get a room for next Monday. Take this number and call me. I'll have the money delivered to you at that room by two guys. I will not be with them. It will be in three liquor cartons, so take your time when it's delivered."

"I understand, Sonny," Jim said. "I'll give the winning ticket to the guys when they deliver the money."

"Okay," said Condo.

That evening, Jim started thinking that having the ticket on him when the guys came with the money was maybe not such a good idea. Suppose they had the cartons loaded with cut-up newspaper? Just as they walk into the hotel room, suppose they put the cartons down and ask to see the ticket? When the ticket is produced, they'll pull guns, take the ticket and then they'll tie us up or even shoot us. *Who knows what these guys may try to pull,* Jim thought. *I think we better find another way to close this deal. What can I do?*

Mae didn't say a word. She knew her husband well enough to know the wheels were turning.

Chapter

Unknown to Jim, when he went to the meeting on 23rd street, he and the guy who approached him were being watched and followed by two FBI agents.

When Jim did not want to talk to this guy, the guy walked back to his car and drove away. The two FBI agents decided that one of them would drive after the car containing the ex-con, who was well known to the police and the FBI as a dope pusher. The other FBI agent got out of the car and followed Jim, keeping him under strict surveillance. Jim walked west on 23rd Street and then south on 8th Avenue. The FBI had been trained to stay as close as possible and to be unnoticed by anybody. He looked like a man just out for a walk. When they got to Jim's street and walked west, the FBI agent noticed a lady looking out of her window and she waved to Jim. She did seem to be very anxious. The FBI agent watched Jim go into a tenement apartment house.

After the FBI agent made note of all of this activity in his logbook, he then contacted his headquarters.

His partner kept the other suspect under surveillance and watched him go into a restaurant in lower Manhattan.

After the agents reported back to headquarters, they went over the possible deal that had just occurred. They knew the suspect very well. His name was Louis Crumb and the police and FBI always keep a close eye on him, knowing what a wheeler and dealer this guy is.

Now the FBI wanted to know why Crumb stopped and talked to this man on 23rd Street and 7th Avenue in New York City.

The agent, who followed Jim to his apartment house on the west side and learned his name, looked up the FBI files and contacted the New York City police to see if they had any record on him.

Well, Jim came up very clean. The agents decided that they would pay a visit to Jim's apartment and see if they could learn just why Jim met this guy Crumb.

The agents knocked on Jim's door very early the next morning. They identified themselves and asked Jim if they could come in and talk to him. Jim hesitated for a minute because, as somewhat of a wise guy, he figured that these guys could be phonies passing for FBI agents.

Jim said, "Wait a minute. You wake a man up out of a sound sleep and you just want to ask a few questions. How do I know that you are FBI agents?"

They started to laugh and said, "Here, look at our credentials." Jim asked if they had identification with their name and the FBI's phone number. They asked why he wanted that. Jim told them to wait in the hall while he called their office to make sure that they were legit.

By this time, Mae could not help but hear all of this. She got up and came to the door. Jim told her to stay inside and he would be right there. Jim made the phone call. He asked about these two agents. He gave them the men's names and the office confirmed that they were in fact FBI agents.

Jim went back to the door and told the agents to come in. They proceeded to enter the apartment and told Jim that they were going to show him a few pictures to see if he knew any of these people.

The first picture was of Louis Crumb with a number on his chest. "Do you know this man?"

Jim said, "No."

"Are you sure?"

"I have never seen him in my life. I don't know who he is."

They said, "Be very careful and make sure that you do not make up any lies. Just tell the truth. Do you know the man in this picture?"

" No."

"Well then," the FBI agent said, "we better take you to our headquarters and we will show you a few more pictures to see if they refresh your memory."

Mae asked, "Is Jim was under arrest?"

"No."

"Should I call a lawyer?"

"That's probably not necessary. We are only going to look at a few pictures and Jim can answer any questions we have. He'll be home in a few hours."

Their car was parked at the door in front of the building. Jim did not like the idea of going out the door with these guys because the neighbors would know the law when they saw them.

When they arrived at the FBI headquarters, they escorted Jim up to their office. Jim was told to take a seat and relax until they would be able to show him some mug shots.

The first picture they showed him was Crumb's. Again, Jim said that he did not know him. They told him, "Jim, we will tell you what we know and then we want you to tell us what you know, okay?" Jim told them to go ahead.

"You were standing on a corner at 23rd and 7th at about 9 P.M. last night when a car pulled up and Crumb went over and talked to you. Now," they said, "the question is very simple. What did he want? What did he say?"

Jim said, "In the first place, I do not remember that guy or what he looked like. I only talked to him less than a minute and I don't even know what he looks like."

The agents said, "Okay, Jim, you don't know what he looks like and you could not pick him out of a line up, but the question is what did he say to you? What did he want?"

"I don't remember."

They repeated, "You don't remember? A guy stops a car, gets out, goes over to you and says something, but you don't remember?"

"That's right," Jim said.

"We are employed by the United States Federal Government and we do not go around harassing people or bothering anyone who does not break the law. We know this guy Crumb very well. He is an ex-convict and he knows and associates with some very bad people. Dope is his main support and we are going to get him. The next time we do, he is going to go away for a long time."

Jim said, "That is his hard luck."

They said, "You can say that again, and that goes for anyone who has anything to do with him." They told Jim to sit there while they went over a few things and they would get back to him when they could.

After almost two hours, one of the agents came back into the office where Jim was still sitting and he said to Jim, "You can go home. If we ever want to talk you again, we will give you a call."

After Jim left the building, he took his time. He wanted to think and maybe drop the whole idea. He might even tell Condo what a punk deal that he tried to set up for him. He kept going over what he would tell Condo and all of the so-called wise guys.

As Jim was walking home, he started to think about not telling Condo anything. Mae is more than fed up with this whole idea. So, maybe I should not tell Condo anything. If he calls and asks, I'll just say that I am not interested. If he just wants to meet me for the pay off for the lotto ticket, I'll just say, let's set up a date and place and it better be soon, he thought.

During this time, the girls were in touch with each other and they called their mother to see how she and Dad were. Mae was so upset. She told them that the FBI had questioned Jim and taken him to their office for more questions and to look at more pictures. Mae told the girls that the FBI agents had taken Dad at 8 A.M. and now it was almost 12 P.M. and still no word from Dad.

Jim finally came home while Mae was on the phone with her daughters. He took the phone, told them about everything, and explained that he did not even know who the guy was. Jim told the girls that he did not want to talk any more on the phone and he would wait until the next time they were all together. He said he would show them what a big joke this whole thing was and then said good-bye.

When Jim got off the phone, he turned to Mae and told her that he knew he was giving her a hard time about this big idea he had. He told her he didn't blame her if she did not want to hear anymore about it.

Mae asked what they had done to him. "Did they hurt you in any way?" Jim said that they had actually been friendly, had asked a few questions and he answered them.

Mae asked, "What are you going to do now?"

Jim said, "Nothing as of right now. I'm not even going to call Condo."

"Are you hungry?" Mae asked.

"I'll have a sandwich and some tea." He was still a little shook up.

While Jim and Mae were having lunch, Mae asked Jim about the photo that the FBI agents showed him. "Was he the man you met on 23rd Street?" Mae asked.

Jim said, "Yes, he was the one."

"What did you say to the FBI agents?"

"I just told them that I did not remember him or what he said. I would not be surprised to hear from the FBI again."

Mae could not help but say again how she wished that Jim would just turn in the lotto ticket and take whatever he wins.

Jim said, "I told you before that I should have listened to you and now I am saying it again. You are right." The phone rang and it was one of the girls asking if everything was okay.

"Yes. Dad has just gotten back from the FBI headquarters and he is having some lunch." Jim hollered to Mae that she shouldn't stay on the phone any longer.

While Jim was watching television a few days later, he watched a scene about a big drug bust in Queens, New York and to his surprise, there was Louis Crumb being put into a police van. Jim got excited and said, "There is the dirty bum. I'm glad that the police arrested him. I hope the judge throws the book at him and he rots in jail with all the rest of them."

Mae said, "You know that you are just as bad as they are." Jim could not believe his ears and asked Mae what she meant. She said, "You are trying to sell your winning ticket, not pay any taxes and cheat the government and the state, isn't that right?"

Jim said, "Boy, this is getting bad. I'm having a problem with Condo, then the FBI and now you."

Mae said, "I'm just telling you what you are doing, or are willing to do, when you get involved with all of these hoodlums."

Jim told Mae, "You are right and I wish that I had never gotten this idea of getting all this money and not having to pay any taxes. With the money, I dreamed that we could split it with the kids and they all could pay off all their bills and live a better life. That was what the whole idea was about. Now, I won't be surprised if the FBI calls me to ask more questions."

Sure enough, at approximately 10 A.M. the next day, the phone rang and the FBI asked Jim to come over to their office. They said they wanted to ask him more questions and suggested that he could be a witness for the government. Jim took his time going over to the FBI office. He figured that if the FBI really wanted him, they would have come to his home and taken him to their office. He felt that it would be just a routine thing and he would stick to his story. He would tell them that he didn't know Crumb, didn't recognize him and could not remember what was said on the corner of 23rd Street. He would tell them he was just out for a walk.

When Jim finally got to the FBI office, they showed him into a room and they were very cordial. They said, "Let's go over a few things first. You were on the corner of 23rd Street and 7th Avenue the other night when this guy Crumb got out of his car and talked to you. Now you have to admit that's right."

Jim answered, "I was continuing my walk when a car stopped. I don't know who the guy was or what he had to say. I was not interested in listening to him I did not want to bother with the guy."

"Why weren't you interested in talking to this guy? Maybe he just wanted information or maybe directions to the Holland Tunnel. Let's stop kidding each other. You knew what he wanted and maybe you are not the only one."

"I did not pay any attention to the guy."

"Why not?"

Jim said, "You know that is a bad area with pimps and prostitutes, so how would I know who this guy was or why would I care? I was just out for a walk and that is all there is to it."

The agent said, "Listen, we have a good case against this guy and he is locked up right now. We will go to trial and we are going to do all that we can to get him convicted and sent to prison for the rest of his life."

"That is your business."

"We think that there are more people involved and the FBI intends to get to the bottom of it. When we do, Jim, don't say that we didn't try to warn you."

"Warn me about what? If I tell you that I don't know the guy, what more do I have to say?"

The agent said, "Let us assure you that we will find the truth sooner or later. As a matter of fact, it may come from Crumb himself when he faces life in prison, like all the rest of the wise guys, he will look to make a deal for himself. When he does, and you can bet your life on it, he will pour his guts out to try to save himself. Don't think that there is any honor among these guys. They would rat on their own mother. We'll let you sit here and think it over for a while." Jim sat there and just kept thinking how he wished that he had listened to Mae and the kids. They did not like the idea at all. He kept saying to himself if he tells these guys the truth, he knew that he would get into trouble. He thought about a court trial and lawyers. What a mess.

After about two hours, as Jim sat alone in the office, two agents came in, looked at him and said, "So how is it going? We gave you a very nice chance to think it over. Are you going to help us?"

Jim answered, "I told you all that I can. There is nothing else that I can say."

They said, "Okay Jim, we are going to let you go home again, just like the other day. Here are our cards in case you change your mind or remember anything that can help us. Give us a call. Keep in mind that we will get to the bottom of this. You might as well know that you may be called as a material witness even though you did not give us a statement. Bear in mind, you may still go to court. So, if you do not have anything else to tell us, go ahead and leave."

On the way home, Jim was very upset. He certainly did not want to go to court. Then he said to himself, *If I did tell the FBI why I met that guy on 23rd Street, then they surely would make me take the stand. So, at least this way they may never call me.*

When Jim got home again he went over the situation with Mae. He told her that he would keep his eye on the television news and the daily paper and see when this guy Crumb is going to go to trial. It certainly is serious since the judge held Crumb without bail. He is a three-time loser. Now the question is, is Crumb going to keep his own mouth shut or will he try to make a deal as the FBI agents said he would?

"I sure got myself in some mess," Jim told Mae. Jim told Mae and the girls not to call each other about the matter since the phone might be tapped. After a few days passed, Jim was staying home and not doing anything about the lotto ticket. He wanted to try to relax a little. A week passed and nobody seemed to be doing anything. No word from the Feds or even Condo.

Chapter 19

Bill, Jim's son-in-law, was having lunch one afternoon in a restaurant downtown when Chinatown Harry came over and gave him a pay phone number. He told Bill that Jim should call that number from another pay phone either in a candy store or a drug store on Monday night at 9 P.M. because Condo wanted to talk to him. Bill did not want to deliver the message at Jim's house because it would be taking him out of his way on his way home from work, so he decided to type out a letter and mail it to Jim and let Jim decide what he wanted to do about calling Condo.

When Jim received Bill's letter, he was quite surprised and asked Mae, "Now what does he want to do?" On Monday evening, Jim went out for a walk, stopped into a drug store about 9 P.M., and made the call. Condo picked up right away. He asked Jim how he was doing and Jim said, "Okay, but a little annoyed."

Condo said, "I'm glad that you keep quiet about these things. Actually, I have a better idea for you."

Jim asked, "Like what?"

Condo said, "We will meet soon to make the payoff for the lotto ticket. I would like for you to hold on to some ready cash. Once in a while, me and my friends may need some cash right away and if we do, we would always give you the same interest that any guy would pay a loan shark or any moneylender. It will not be compounded interest. If I need $20,000, I will give you $25,000 back in thirty days. It will always be just one payment. With all this money on hand, it might be a good idea to be a moneylender."

After hearing all of this, Jim asked, "Is that all?"

Condo said, "Yeah. The swap will be made soon for the lotto ticket."

Jim said, "Okay. I'll wait to hear from you again."

As Jim walked out of the drug store, two FBI agents said, "Hello Jim. "How are you? What is the matter? Is your phone at home out of order?"

Jim said, "No. I just wanted to say something to one of the kids while I thought of it."

The next day, Jim got a call from the FBI agents who told him that the U.S. Attorney wanted to put him on the stand at Crumb's trial. "Be ready for a call to report to the Federal Courthouse at Foley Square," the agent said.

Chapter 20

Mae received a call from a very dear friend of hers who lived in Greenwich Village. "Would you and Jim like to come down for supper on Friday night?" her friend asked.

Mae answered, "That would be very nice. We'll be there about 7 P.M."

Mae told Jim that she had made the date to go to their friend's house on Perry Street for supper on Friday night. Jim thought that would be great. On Friday, Mae commented, "The weather is so nice. Let's walk down to Perry Street."

After they visited their friend and had a nice fish dinner, they watched "Keeping Up" on television. Jim, Mae and their friend always watched this show because the show was very funny. After saying good night, Jim suggested that they walk to Abingdon Square and get the bus up 8th Avenue. By this time, it was about 11 P.M. As they arrived at their bus stop, they noticed a lot of people in front of the tenement building.

Mae said, "Look at all of these people. Whatever is the matter?"

They arrived in front of their house and asked the neighbors what was the matter. The neighbors all started to talk at the same time. The electricity was out in their building and this was the only building affected on the whole block. The police and the electric company had been called and they were trying to find out where the problem was. Jim and Mae stayed and talked to their neighbors. One neighbor told them that the electricity had been off since around 10 P.M. Another neighbor asked if they had watched "Keeping Up." Mae said, "Yes. It was very funny."

As they were talking, Jim was thinking what might have really happened here. One of the neighbors said that they had seen a strange man in the building around 8 P.M. Jim suspected that something was about to happen. Maybe someone was trying to get him in the dark.

All of a sudden, the lights went on in the hall and the police and workmen from the electric company told everyone that things seemed to be okay now. They found shorts in the wires in the back yard.

By this time, Jim's mind was racing. *The shorts, the strange man, the whole house was completely dark . . . something is going on.* Jim was worried and he said to Mae, "Let's be very careful. I will go into the apartment first and make sure it is okay."

Mae suggested, "We should ask the police to stay until we check out our apartment."

"That's a good idea. I'll run and ask the police to stay just a little longer."

When Jim and Mae first arrived home, one of the neighbors was talking about watching the television news at 6 P.M. She had seen a story about a drug bust. The trial would be starting soon and all of these dope pushers were being held without bail.

Jim said, "The news report sounds very interesting. It would be great if the police could remove all of the drug pushers off the street once and for all. The city, the state and the whole country should be free of these dope pushers."

As Jim and Mae entered their apartment, Jim said to Mae, "What a relief. No more trouble."

"What do you mean?"

Jim said, "I have to see what the FBI is going to do."

Chapter 21

The trial for Crumb began again on Monday. This was the third day of the trial. Jim, accompanied by two of his daughters, arrived at the courthouse on time and was told to sit in a room where there were two more witnesses for the prosecution. Nobody talked. One witness was called first. At about 11:30 A.M., Jim was called. The U.S. Attorney got right to the point after Jim was sworn in. He said, "You just swore to tell the truth and the whole truth. Do you understand?"

"Of course," Jim answered.

"Were you on the corner of 23rd Street and 7th Avenue in New York City on the night of October 15th?"

Jim answered, "Yes. I was out for a walk and I usually walk up in that neighborhood."

"Now," the Government lawyer asked, "do you know this defendant, Louis Crumb?"

Jim said, "No, I do not know him."

"Did this man get out of a car, walk over to you and ask you some questions?"

Jim answered, "I do not remember."

The U.S. Attorney asked the judge, "May I treat this witness as hostile?"

The judge replied, "No you may not."

"Your Honor, this man is hiding something and we want an answer."

"This witness answered that he did not remember seeing or talking to the defendant, so get on with your next question."

"I have no more questions for him."

The judge excused Jim and Jim walked out of court followed by the two daughters.

Jim's daughters said, "Oh thank God, Dad. We were so frightened for you."

Jim said, "I have to admit that the judge was very lenient with me. I think he could have gotten pretty rough, but I guess he knows the law or else he might have thrown me in the can for a few days. I am glad it is over. I better go home. Your mother must be worried."

Jim was always worried about when the FBI would contact him. He was sure that they were not finished with him. Sure enough, a few days later, the FBI called and told Jim to come to their office at 10 A.M. the next morning.

Jim could not sleep all night. Early in the morning, he got out of bed and fixed the coffee for breakfast. Mae awoke and asked, "Why are you up so early?"

"I couldn't sleep."

She said, "Yes, I knew that you were very restless. Try not to worry. Maybe they will just ask you a few questions and then let you go home."

"I hope so."

When Jim arrived at FBI Headquarters, he was ushered into a room where two agents got right to the point. They told Jim that they were going to ask him again about what Crumb had said to him as he got out of his car on 23rd Street and 7th Avenue. "Tell us exactly what words were spoken."

"I do not remember Crumb or anything he had to say. How can I tell you something that I do not remember?"

"The Government had a good case against these dope pushers and most likely they will be put away for the rest of their lives. If you are a good citizen, you should be glad to cooperate with us and get these guys off the streets."

"I don't remember seeing this guy, what he looked like and what he said."

"We don't believe you."

"I'm very sorry, but I cannot help you."

"We are going to show you more pictures to see if you know any of the people." They started to produce all kinds of pictures. Jim did recognize a few of them, including Condo, but he kept saying that he didn't recognize any of them.

Jim must have looked at five hundred photos and he was getting tired of seeing so many photos. He repeated over and over that he did not remember anybody's picture or know any one of them.

"Do you read the daily newspapers?"

"Yes, of course."

They asked, "How about the news on television? Do you watch the news?"

Again Jim said, "Yes, but I don't know or recognize any of these people."

Jim was getting tired, so he just sat there and said no more. The agents were in and out of the office quite often. Jim just sat there. "Okay," they said to Jim, "the U.S. Attorney wants to talk to you and we advise you to tell him the truth."

Jim thought that he would have to get a lawyer. It looked like these guys meant business and he was getting tired, but if he told them anything, then he surely would be in hot water with them and maybe Condo.

The young U.S. Attorney came into the room and introduced himself. He said, "You were on the corner of 23rd Street and 7th Avenue in New York City when a car stopped and a man got out. He went over to you and after a minute or so, got back into his car and drove away. Is that right?"

Jim said, "I don't remember."

He asked, "You don't remember a man, a car or anything that was said or even what he looked like?"

Jim replied, "Maybe it all happened so fast that I just don't recall."

The U.S. Attorney said, "Well, we think that you do know!"

Jim said, "I am not going to lie or make up any story for anybody. I can't remember anything that was said."

"Okay, we are going to let you go home, but keep in mind that we will call you again."

"Don't leave town."

"I am not going anywhere," he said, and left the office.

One of the FBI agents said to the U.S. Attorney, "Maybe we have him all wrong. Maybe he really doesn't remember anything."

The other agent remarked, "I think something was said between Jim and Crumb. Whatever it was, maybe some day we will find out."

The U.S. Attorney said, "I'm not sure. He also said that he was not afraid of the court or anyone. It looks like we have a tough cookie on our hands."

As Jim walked home, he was really starting to boil. *Should I talk to a lawyer? If I do, I'll have to tell him what this is all about, especially the lotto ticket. Then the lawyer would want his fee and how much would that be? If I wind up in court, I could blow that lotto ticket money on lawyers.*

Jim was very hungry. Mae fixed lunch and even a highball. She said, "Here, drink this and try to relax."

Jim told Mae, "You know, you are sticking with me a lot more than I deserve."

Mae answered, "I know that you are trying to be good to the whole family, but I certainly will be glad when this whole thing is over and we can get back to normal. What did the U.S. Attorney have to say?"

Jim explained about the questioning and the possibility that he was still under surveillance by the FBI.

Chapter 22

The next day Jim got up out of bed, went into the living room and sat there. Jim started thinking about Condo's lawyer, who always just happened to be claiming what an honest man Condo was. *So, how would it be to have someone give this guy the ticket when the call was made to deliver the dough? In other words, why not have Bill go to the lawyer's office to deliver the ticket and have him call Condo when he had the ticket, and then Condo could deliver the money. The lawyer couldn't pull a fast one because he would never want to get involved and face the possibility of being found out and getting disbarred. Disbarment was certainly more important to those guys than anything. I'll get in touch with Condo and tell him that this is how it will be worked. Bill will deliver the ticket to Condo's lawyer, and the lawyer will contact Condo. Condo, in the meantime, will have called me at the hotel so that his guys can leave the money and go. One other thing,* Jim thought, *I'll have Susan call for three rooms at the hotel for the family to stay on either side of us. They will stay quiet and out of the way, keeping their doors shut. After the delivery, we can open each room from the inside and split up the money to be carried out of the hotel. We will not go out together. Dave and Ed can bring their cars and park at the garage. We could, Mae and I, get a cab and go up to Susan and Dave's house on Gunn Hill Road. From there, we can figure out how we can best handle the rest of the way. Yes,* Jim thought, *that would be the best way to make the transfer of the money. Then I think we better go somewhere where we can relax, after all of this business is settled. We better not come back to this flat, because someone could be watching us. And, we better not go back to any of the kids' apartments for the same reason. I wonder if we could all go up to the Poconos? As a matter of fact, next Thursday is Thanksgiving, so if we make the deal on Monday, why not go right up to the mountains for the rest of the week, kids and all. They would have to take off from their jobs, and even take the grandchildren out of school, but the little guys would love that. We could go up to the mountains, spend a nice five or six days; have a good Thanksgiving dinner with no work for the women. All of us would just have a nice time, a few drinks. At night, they have music at the lounge. We could all have a ball. In the morning, we will call the kids so that they can make arrangements with their jobs and schools. We will call for reservations. Now, Jim thought, I can go back to bed, get some sleep and feel much better about the outlook as these things finally start to take place.*

Jim told Mae, "I think the first thing I will have to do is to call Sonny and tell him about my idea of having the lotto ticket delivered to his lawyer's office. He can call Sonny and tell him when everything is okay."

At 10 A.M., Jim gave Sonny a call. After explaining to Sonny how the winning ticket would be delivered to his lawyer's office, Sonny did not like the idea.

"I don't like to let everybody, no matter who they are, know everything that I'm doing."

"Sonny, I can't just hand over the ticket to a couple of guys who'll come to the room at the hotel."

"Look, Jim, all you have to do is open the cartons, count the money, and give them the ticket and then they'll be on their way. Let's keep this as simple as possible. Nothing will go wrong. Don't be afraid that these guys will try to pull anything. The guys will come to the room at the hotel, put down the money, let you count it, take the winning lotto ticket and leave."

"Okay, Sonny," Jim said. "On Monday, I will call you to let you know what room number that I'm in. One other thing, Sonny. I want you to know that my wife will be with me at that time, and maybe I better have a little protection with me just in case. Even after I leave the hotel, carrying all of that dough is a big risk."

"All I know," Sonny answered, "is that I will have the money at the hotel. The rest is up to you. That has nothing to do with me. Our deal will be over just as soon as you get the money and I get the ticket."

"Okay, Sonny," Jim said. "I'll call you Monday afternoon."

The only thing now, Jim thought, *is to make sure that Ed and Dave are both listening from the rooms so they can step in just in case this deal goes sour.*

Mae and Jim called Susan, Dolly and Nancy and told each of them what was going to take place. They were very agreeable except that they didn't like having the kids miss any school. Jim assured them that it was only for a couple of days and if they needed an excuse, for them to tell their teachers that their grandfather croaked and they have to go to the funeral.

The girls did not think that was so funny, but they each said that they'd take care of the schools. Jim told Susan to call the hotel for reservations. She assured him that she would. Jim suggested to all of them that perhaps they'd better get together on Saturday or Sunday just to go over a few plans and make sure everything would be all right. They agreed to that.

Jim told Mae that he would go out and buy six money belts for each one of them to wear and carry as much money in them as possible. That would mean less that they would have to put into their traveling bags. Jim went to an old Army Navy store where they sold money belts.

The storekeeper told Jim, "You know, there's an awful lot of people buying these belts lately. I guess people are getting sick and tired of being robbed."

"Yes," Jim said, "I think people are getting fed up."

When Jim got back, Mae said, "Dolly called back and said that she had called Nancy and Susan and asked them to meet at her house with us on Saturday and to stay for dinner. I told her that was fine."

Jim took a walk to find Chick Thompson and Butch Dunlevy to ask them to be at the hotel on Monday. He told them to arrive at 5 P.M. and to wait in the lobby. He told them he'd be up in the hotel and would look for them when he came down. He explained to them that he'd be taking a cab with Mae and for them to ride up to Susan's house in the Bronx and, of course, there would be a few hundred dollars in it for each of them. They both agreed that it sounded good and they would be at the hotel before 5 P.M.

Chapter 23

On Saturday afternoon, Jim and Mae took the subway to Bayridge, Brooklyn to Ed and Dolly's house. They were there before Nancy and Susan. Jim and Ed sat around watching some college football games. When the others came, they waited until after supper to go over their plans. They could not help but mention a few things during the game, so when they finished eating, it was already pretty settled as to what they would do. Jim stressed as forcefully as he could that each of them would be getting five hundred thousand dollars. He told them to not go wacky and do anything foolish, to use the money as prudently as possible. They all agreed. Dave, Ed and Bill said that they would stay on their jobs, in spite of the money. All of them had many years of seniority and could look forward to a pension.

"When we get up to the Poconos, we'll buy a brand new Ford station wagon. That's one car I always admired," Jim said.

Everyone laughed. Dave said, "Why not? But do you know how to drive a car?"

"Sure I do," Jim said. "It has been a long time, so while you're all up there with us, we can drive around and I'll get used to driving again."

Soon it was Monday. The big day had finally arrived. Jim and Mae were both very anxious. They nervously had breakfast and packed bags.

"You did tell Mrs. Smith to get our mail and watch out for the house, didn't you?" Jim asked.

"I took care of everything," Mae assured him.

They left their apartment at 2 P.M. and walked to the corner where they hailed a cab. Jim gave the driver their destination. When they arrived at the hotel, Jim went right up to the clerk, paid for the rooms for the day and got the keys. They went up to the room and put the television on. They heard Susan and Dave in the next room, and a few minutes later, from the opposite side, they heard Ed and Dolly in theirs. Jim's heart was pumping very fast. "I'll be glad when this is over," he said. Mae agreed.

Jim called Sonny. "We're in room 621."

"That's great," Sonny said. "My friends will be there at about 4 P.M. with the money."

At 4 P.M. on the dot, there was a knock on the door. Jim answered. Two guys stood there. "Are you Jim?" one asked.

"Yes," Jim answered, his heart racing.

They came in with three old liquor cartons, just as Sonny had said. The cartons were tied up with heavy cord. They put the cartons on the bed, opened them, and spread the money out on the bedspread. They told Jim that he could look the money over and start to count it.

"Give me a hand," Jim asked Mae. As they counted it, they packed it back into the cartons. The two guys just stood there and never said a word. Jim and Mae finished counting and repacking and were satisfied that the money was all there. Jim wanted to give the guys a tip, but they both said that all they were told to do is deliver the money, get the lotto ticket, and leave. No tip was necessary.

"Okay," Jim told them. Suit yourself." He gave them the winning ticket. "I'm finally getting rid of this. Boy, am I glad."

The men wished Jim and Mae good luck and were on their way.

A moment later, Susan, Dave, Dolly and Ed opened the connecting doors into Jim and Mae's room. They all looked extremely relieved.

"You know," said Ed, "I was starting to really shake, because if those guys ever did try to pull a fast one, most likely they'd have guns. What a mess that would turn out to be."

"Yes," said Jim, "but everything went smooth. So let's get this money into the belts and the leftover into our traveling bags. We can leave our keys in the rooms and just walk out. Your mother and I will leave first. Chick and Butch will be waiting for us in the lobby. Then you leave the way you came. We'll get a cab with Chick and Butch and go up to your place. You meet us there. Drive carefully, and take it easy. I want to take a few hundred dollar bills and put it into my pocket so I can stake Chick and Butch and they can then take the same cab right back downtown."

All of this had gone like clockwork. Jim gave Chick and Butch two hundred and an extra fifty to take care of the cab when they got back downtown. Ed and Dolly drove back to Brooklyn to pick up their children and head up to the Poconos. After Jim and Mae paid off Chick and Butch, they proceeded to collect Susan, Dave and their kids and then drove up in Dave's car to the mountains.

They arrived quite late and had a snack and a few drinks. Nancy and Bill came up the next day. Jim was very anxious to get out to a Ford dealer to buy his new station wagon and Dave and Ed went to the dealer with him. The car would be ready for him the next day. He told the salesman that this was a cash buy and wanted the best deal that the salesman could give him.

"Don't worry," the salesman said. "I'll give you the best deal that you'll find anywhere. We cannot be beat," he assured Jim.

Jim, Ed and Dave drove back to the hotel. The grandchildren were playing outside and when Bill and Nancy pulled into the grounds, everyone got all excited. The youngsters ran to Bill's car with great excitement. Everyone helped Bill and Nancy unload their car. Everyone was talking at once, telling them how Pop had bought a new Ford station wagon.

They went into the dining room for some lunch. The staff at the hotel arranged for a table for the children right next to the adults. They talked about the cash and Jim told them, out of earshot of the children, to use the money belts as much as possible. They all agreed.

"The rest of the cash might be better off left in the trunks of the cars. You can never tell if the cleaning people will find it," he told them. "Start to put as much as you can, as soon as you can, into the banks, CDs, savings or checking accounts." They agreed to do this.

"Mae," Jim said, "after we pick up the station wagon tomorrow, I'd like to go to a real estate office to see if we can find a nice house up here. I always liked those ads that are in the papers about the Poconos, so let's see if we can find ourselves such a place."

Chapter 24

As Chick and Butch rode back downtown to the West side, Chick remarked, "I wonder what kind of a deal that Jim fell into giving us that kind of cash."

"Yeah," Butch said, "it is very interesting, but whatever it is, I wish him luck. After all, it didn't cost us anything and we grabbed a good day's pay for it."

Chick said, "I think that Jim must have said something or fell into some kind of an inheritance and the people who they were doing business with are staying at the Story."

Butch said, "I guess it has to be some kind of a deal like that, but maybe they hit the lotto and were just collecting the money from the hotel where these lotto people may have an office."

Chick said, "Well, whatever it is, I wish them good luck."

• • •

The rest of that Tuesday went very well. After dinner, the adults sat around and talked while the kids watched television. There were some copies of the New York papers that they looked at, but no one could concentrate too much on reading.

Everyone got up early on Wednesday. They all had their own cabins, close to each other. Little by little, they drifted outside to get some fresh air and sunshine and went into the dining room for breakfast.

Bill had a *New York Post* and, as he was glancing through it, he found a short story about Sonny Condo hitting the lotto. Bill got all excited and said, "Hey, look at this! A story about Condo hitting the lotto for $4,000,000."

"Where? Where?" asked Jim.

"Here in the *Post*," Bill said. "Boy, isn't that hot stuff."

Everyone laughed hard. The kids were all wondering what was so funny.

"Oh, just something we read in the paper," Mae told them.

"You know," Jim said, "this will probably be on television tonight." Everyone agreed to watch the news.

"The paper says," Bill told them, "that he would have claimed the money sooner, but he wanted to think about what he would do with his lucky winnings. Condo is quoted as saying, 'Boy is this going to be a great Thanksgiving'." Everyone broke up laughing again.

"Come on, Mom," Jim said to Mae, "let's get started and go and get our car."

"The car won't be ready until after 2 P.M. The dealer said that he'd get you temporary plates and get the car ready," Dave reminded him.

"What time is it now?" Jim asked.

"10 A.M."

"Okay," Jim said. "I guess we have a few hours to kill. If any of the rest of you want to go any place or do anything, go right ahead. Just be careful and don't let anybody sell you anything that you don't need or want. As soon as we get the car today, your mother and I are going to look for a house."

That afternoon, Dave drove Mae and Jim to the car dealer. The car was ready and waiting. After Jim paid the salesman, the salesman wished them the best of luck. Jim told Dave to return to the hotel and that he and Mae would drive around and look at some property.

They returned around 6 P.M. Mae was the first one to announce that they found a nice house. It was on lovely grounds near a lake. "The whole place is very nice and ready to move into," she said. "We gave the real estate man a $5,000 deposit and told him to close the deal as soon as possible. He told us that he would be back on Friday to show all of us how nice the house is and to see if you like it as much as we do."

Bill interrupted their excitement. "Come see the news and see if they show Condo getting the lotto check."

"Sure enough, here comes the big ham now," said Jim. "Look at him. What an actor. He should get an Oscar for this performance. Here he is, saying how he bought the ticket last

September, but he just did not want to rush into anything. Now he says he'll go away for a nice vacation."

Dave said, "Gee. I hope he doesn't come up here." Everybody had a hard laugh at that.

"Condo said what a great Thanksgiving he's going to have. Well, this will be our greatest Thanksgiving," Jim said.

On Friday, Jim tried to fit everyone in his new station wagon, but it was just a little too much. Ed and his family followed in their car. Jim and Mae were anxious to show them their new home. The kids loved it. They were all asking if they would have a horse, chickens and even a cow. Jim told them, "Sure, we'll have everything, even a nice big police dog."

On Saturday, all the kids left the hotel for their own homes. Jim and Mae decided to stay for a few weeks more to close the deal on the house and to buy some furniture and other things they'd need. This way, he and Mae could actually stay at their own house. This was the first home they ever owned. They shopped happily, buying many things that they would need. They found a nice bedroom set and a kitchen table and chairs that would be sent from the store as soon as possible. They started to fix up the house right away.

Jim began hiding a lot of the money under the floorboards. They had opened some bank accounts in banks up in the Poconos. "What are we going to do with the flat on the west side?" he asked Mae.

"I think we'll keep it for now until we know best what to do."

"Okay," Jim agreed, "and when we leave here and go home, maybe we can look at real estate ads in the papers and see if there's a nice place down in Florida for us."

"All that I will be doing is fixing up houses to live in," Mae said.

"Yes, but look at all the fun that you'll be having," he said.

"Most likely, the kids will want to be getting places of their own."

"That's just what I want them to do," Jim said. "To get places of their own. I want them to do anything that they want to do, just as long as they do not get into any bum deals, whether it's buying a house or anything else. I know they are all very sensible and I'm sure that they just won't go out and blow the dough on anything foolish."

Chapter 25

When they returned to the city, Jim added a few deposits to his existing bank accounts, including his checking account, where he deposited as much cash money that he could without drawing attention to himself. He also opened a lot of new accounts in other banks. Jim and Mae kept in contact with the kids to see how they were doing with the money they had. They wanted to know if the kids were opening bank accounts for themselves and the grandchildren. Everything was going smoothly.

One day while Mae was looking at the real estate ads for Florida, she noticed an ad for a house, fully furnished, located in Beverly Hills, Florida. It had a New York number to call. She told Jim about it.

"Let's give them a call," he said, excited, then picked up the phone. When he hung up, he said, "It turns out that these people inherited the house from their parents, who passed away. They're asking $65,000, fully furnished. I asked them if that's rock bottom, and the guy said that if we were really interested, he would come down to sixty. I told him that it sounded good and asked him to set up an appointment to meet and close the deal. I told him that we'd like to get the house as soon as possible because we'd like to be in Florida for the winter. He told me it would be okay and he'd call his lawyer and get back to us in a day or so. I gave him our number."

The next day, the man called and gave Mae the details to meet at his lawyer's office and close the deal on that Saturday morning. Mae told him that she and Jim would be there.

Jim and Mae called a young friend of the family who had just become a lawyer to go with them to close the deal. He agreed to meet them at the sellers' attorney's office in midtown Manhattan.

Jim took his checkbook and a lot of cash with him. He didn't want his lawyer or the other people to ask too many questions. If they did, Jim would tell them that he had been very lucky at the track.

No one was too surprised when they closed the deal for the Florida property. Jim's lawyer told him to hold $10,000 of the $65,000 asking price for an extra ninety days, just in case there were any repairs needed to be made to the house or if any of the appliances needed to be replaced. The sellers and their lawyer had no objections. The people turned over the keys and the deed. The lawyer told Jim to send the balance to him after the ninety days were up.

Chapter

It was December and everyone was busy preparing for Christmas. Jim and Mae would spend Christmas day at Susan's house in the Bronx, as they usually did. Everyone always had dinner and exchanged presents at Susan's. It was a great day for all of them, especially the kids. Santa was good to them.

The day after Christmas, Jim and Mae were all packed and their new station wagon was all set for the road. This was one trip that Jim was looking forward to. He could hit the road, free as a bird, without a trouble in the world. They made two overnight stops on their way south. They both enjoyed the ride and seeing the country. All the way down south, Jim and Mae were very pleased. They found the house and were pleasantly surprised. After they had taken their time and looked the house and property over, Jim started to unload the wagon.

Jim was always very anxious to go out early in the morning for a New York paper to see if there was any more news on the lotto matter. He also wanted to read about how things were going in New York City and especially to see the sports results for boxing and horse racing.

By getting the paper every morning, Jim got to know a few of the fellows who were also from New York and they all hit it off very well. One guy liked to talk to Jim alone and Jim felt the same about him. Hank was kind of a windy guy who loved to spout off about the great wonders that he knew and the big deals he got into. He had also told Jim that he had an interest in a few racehorses and used to box professionally in New York when he was young. He told Jim that he used to box under the name of "News Boy Henry," but because he had a glass chin, most all his fights were knockouts. Hank told Jim that he loved to play cards.

Jim was glad to know that at some time he could sit in on a few card games.

"Some of the guys usually play one and two dollar stakes with no limit on raising," Hank said.

Jim agreed that it sounded good and the next time he and his friends were setting up a game to include him in. "Where do you play?" he asked.

"At the VFW hall, mostly in the afternoons. My wife, Fredna, and I like to go out for dinner on Wednesday and Friday evenings."

"Where do you go out to eat?" Jim asked.

"At a place called the Arrow Restaurant. It has good food and great fish on Fridays," Hank answered.

Through time, Hank, Fredna, Mae and Jim became fast friends. They acted like they'd known each other all their lives. One Friday night, they met Hank and Fredna at the Arrow Restaurant. While having dinner, Jim asked Hank about his racehorses.

Fredna butted right in, "They're all losers. None of them ever even finished in the money. Don't ever waste any money betting on them."

"The stable told me that a few of the horses will be racing at Gulf Stream park and when they do," Hank said, "maybe we can all get together, spend a day at the races and I'll show you around, introduce you to a lot of the trainers and owners and even some jockeys."

"That would be great!" Jim said.

"Jim's just a two dollar better," Mae said. "I never play at all, not even cards."

"That's okay," Hank assured her, "bet anything you want to."

Fredna called Mae in the mornings to ask her to join her and a few friends of hers for lunch or shopping. One day, one of the women had a Tupperware party. Mae loved that. Mae bought a lot of Tupperware and told Jim they could use it not only in Florida, but up in the Poconos.

Hank and Fredna had told Mae and that Jim they originally came from Brooklyn, but lived permanently now in Florida. Jim and Mae never said anything about the lotto, but mentioned they still had their apartment on the west side in New York.

Jim loved the card games with Hank and the other guys. As Hank had said, they were pretty big games and Jim was pretty lucky at winning a few times. He also lost a few. Jim never let on that he had any great amount of money.

One time when the four friends were together, Jim and Mae couldn't help but laugh at a story Hank told about the horses that he had an interest in.

"They couldn't even pull a milk wagon," Fredna said.

"Just wait and see," Hank told her. "Some day I'll have a Kentucky Derby winner."

"That'll be the day," Fredna said.

One day late in January, while Jim was reading the paper, he was startled to see the caption, "Police Checking Story that Condo Bought Winning Lotto Ticket." Jim's heart sank. He called Mae to look at the story in the paper. The article went on to say that the police received a tip that Condo actually had bought the ticket from a winner who did not want to claim the lotto himself, but instead, sold it to Condo.

"The only one who could ever be linked to Condo is Bill because of his talking to that guy, Chinatown Harry." Jim said. "Outside of Bill, I'm the only one who had any contact with Sonny. I hope that nobody tries to give Bill a hard time or ask him any questions."

"I'll give Nancy a call and see if they're okay," Mae said.

"Yes, do that," Jim said.

Mae told Jim that Nancy said she hadn't heard anything about the lotto story and hadn't gotten a chance to read the paper yet.

"Let me talk to her," Jim said. "Nancy, is everything okay?"

"Yes, Pop," Nancy assured him.

"That's good. Now, here's what I want you to do, and tell this to Bill, Dave, Susan, Ed and Dolly. Nobody is to talk to anybody. Do not give anybody any interview or say anything to anyone. If anyone has to take a fall on this, it must be me. As of right now, if worse comes to worst, I think that the only thing they could get me on is tax evasion. If I have to pay a fine or get a lawyer, I will. Do not say anything to anyone. And Nancy, tell Bill to be very careful downtown, especially in that restaurant where he goes for lunch. When you get a chance, tell Bill to give me a call, okay?"

"Okay," Nancy said, "I'll tell him."

Jim put Mae back on the phone and mother and daughter chatted away about other matters.

There was nothing more on television that night about Condo winning the lotto, but the next day reporters were getting very inquisitive. They had found out from the lotto people where the winning ticket for the lotto was sold. It was a candy store on 19th Street and 9th Avenue. A few reporters had gone to the store and asked the owner who it was that he'd sold the winning ticket to. He said that he didn't remember. They asked him if he knew Sonny Condo. He told them he did not. He said that he did not remember who he sold the ticket to and he does not remember everybody who buys a lotto ticket in his store.

Bill called Jim a few days later from his office and told him that the papers in New York City were writing quite a bit about Condo's winning the lotto. Some reporters were asking Condo questions.

Jim told Bill to keep in touch with them and if nothing went wrong and no one started asking any questions, they would stay in Florida as long as they could, or at least until Susan had her baby. Mae wanted to be home for that.

After his conversation with Bill, Jim was very anxious to get the *New York Post* every morning to see if there was anything new on the lotto story and especially to see if the police or the Feds were doing anything. It appeared that the only ones who were interested were the newspaper reporters.

Jim was uneasy for the rest of the day. "We have to be sure to watch the 6 P.M. news and see if they say anything," he said.

When they watched the news, one of the New York announcers said, "Police sources have announced that Sonny Condo bought the winning lotto ticket that he claimed. When asked by reporters if it was true that he bought the lotto ticket from a person who, in fact, was the real winner, Condo's answer was, 'What kind of a nut would sell a winning ticket instead of cashing it in himself? Only a nut would do a thing like that.'" Another reporter called out to Condo and asked, "Where did you buy the winning ticket, Sonny?" Condo answered, "In a candy store on the west side. It's a free country, isn't it?"

Jim said, "That's one thing I never thought of. I should have told Sonny where and when I bought that ticket."

"Doesn't the lotto know where all the tickets are sold?" Mae asked.

"Yes, and that's the reason I should have told Sonny where I got it." He was silent for a minute. "You know who's going to get smart to this now? Butch Dunlevy and Chick Thompson. When they hear about the cops looking into Condo hitting the lotto and buying the winning ticket, they'll put two and two together and they'll figure that it was me who sold the ticket to Condo. Now they'll know why I had them meet me at that hotel. It won't be hard for them to figure out that it was me who actually won the lotto. I do feel that they'll keep it to themselves, though. They're pretty solid guys."

"Yes," Mae said, "until there's money around. Then they'll be just as bad as any one else. Don't be surprised if they want some kind of shakedown in order to keep quiet."

"It's possible," Jim said, "but they never were that kind of people. They were always pretty quiet. Now, of course, the only thing that we can do is take it easy and just continue going as we have been and maybe the whole thing will blow over."

"I wonder if they could do anything to Condo since he will be paying tax on the winning ticket?" Mae asked.

"That's right, if they can't get him, the only one that the law would be interested in is me."

On the weekends, the girls always called Mae and never had anything to report on the matter.

"It's kind of funny when you think of it. Nobody seems to be surprised at all at us buying and paying for a car, a home up in the Poconos and in Florida and always having a lot of money wherever we go," Jim said. "You would think that someone would get smart and start to ask questions."

"Well," Mae said, "I hope not. I don't know when I am ever going to be able to relax."

"Yes. I know what you mean."

Chapter 27

Susan called Mae and Jim. She had been to the doctor and thought that the baby would come around the first week of March. Mae said to Jim, "We'll leave Florida early in March to be back in New York in time for Susan to deliver."

When it was time for them to pack for their return trip to New York, Jim and Mae met with Fredna and Hank for the last time that winter. Hank told Jim to keep in touch and Fredna hated to see Mae leave. They had become real good friends.

"I'll be looking forward to coming down next year," Mae told her, "and we'll have a great winter together."

They left on March 2nd and breezed along Highway 95. They made only one overnight stop and arrived in New York on March 4th.

They unloaded the wagon at the old apartment on the west side and Jim parked the car in a nearby garage. They were finally home.

Jim said, "You know what I've been thinking?"

"I'm afraid to ask," Mae said.

"Well, what I've been thinking is that after the baby is born and the christening is over and everything gets back to normal, I was wondering if, before we go up to the Poconos, we could go for a week or two down to Atlantic City."

"I knew that you would have to come up with a brand new idea," she said. "Why do we need to go to Atlantic City? So you can lose some more money?"

"No! No, no," Jim said. "We can go down and see some good shows and musicals and really live it up. If we do any gambling, it would just be the slots."

"Yes," Mae said, "and how about dice and blackjack? That's what you want to do."

"Okay," Jim said. "After all the celebrations are over and the weather is nice, we can decide then. All right?"

"Sure," Mae answered.

"For the next few days, I'll just hang around, maybe take a walk once in a while and maybe run into Butch and Chick," Jim said.

After a day or two of walking down 8th Avenue, Jim saw Butch and Chick on the corner of 14th Street and 8th Avenue. Jim was happy and surprised to see them. They acted the same way that they always had. Not a word was said or asked about money, the lotto or anything. "How was Florida?" Butch asked.

"Did you and Mae have a nice trip?" Chick asked.

"Everything went very well. We enjoyed ourselves very much," Jim said. "How are you guys doing? You guys all right? Need anything?" They both answered that everything was fine and that they didn't need anything.

When Jim got home, he told Mae how he had met Butch and Chick. He told her how nice they were and they never asked for a thing.

"That's the west side for you, just always real good guys, like the guy who stole the twenty thousand pounds of lumber."

The next morning, Jim and Mae woke up early to begin their day of endless errands. While Mae was in the kitchen preparing breakfast, there was a knock on the door. To Jim and Mae's surprise, two FBI agents stood before them

After some small talk about Jim's trip to Florida, the FBI began to ask questions about how Jim and Mae financed their trip to Florida and their home in the Poconos.

Jim explained to the agents that over the years he had been saving money from his wins at the track. Banks had become too much of a hassle so he had kept the money stashed in drawers and crawl spaces throughout the house.

In an attempt to divert the conversation, Jim invited the two agents to join them for breakfast. While the agents did not accept a meal, they did decide to sit down for a cup of coffee. However, Jim's attempt to change the subject didn't work. The agents informed Jim that he would have to come down to their office because the U.S. Attorney wanted to have a few words with him.

Startled, Jim shouted out, "I didn't know that I was under arrest."

The agents explained that he wasn't, but that there were still unanswered questions that needed to be addressed. With that, Jim got ready and they drove over to the FBI headquarters in an unmarked car.

When they arrived, they took Jim up to a room where Jim was expecting to see the same U.S. Attorney as last time, but this was a different attorney. After brief introductions were made, he asked Jim, "Do you know Sonny Condo?"

Jim replied, "No."

"Well, there seems to be a very suspicious coincidence here. You were seen talking to a guy by the name of Crumb who happens to be a notorious drug pusher and he just happens to be connected to Sonny Condo."

"'But what does this have to do with me?"

"That's what we want to find out" He went on to say, "We are almost certain that Sonny Condo bought a winning lotto ticket from somebody in your neighborhood on 9th Avenue. Then, all of a sudden, you're buying houses, cars and trips and you seem to have plenty of money left. We figure that you have spent over $200,000 already. Now, we would like to know where all of that money came from. So, how about it, Jim. Do you want to tell us where all of this is coming from?"

"I told those agents who just came to my house and drove me here that I always kept a lot of money around the house because I love to gamble. Horses, cards, dice—anything."

Huddling over Jim, the U.S. Attorney asked, "Do you expect me to believe that you've saved over $200,000 from a few card games and then stashed the money in your house? Let me put it to you this way, Jim. We don't believe you. Let me just warn you that we are far from through with this. The Internal Revenue Service is being brought into this to look over your case."

Jim simply replied, "You've gotta do what you've gotta do."

Jim's calm manner only infuriated the attorney who replied, "That's exactly right. I do have to investigate people who are breaking the law. And when we get finished, you better be prepared and get yourself a good lawyer because you're gonna need one, that's for sure! Do you understand that Jim?"

"I sure do. But I don't know of any law that states you have to put your money in the bank!"

"Jim, I think that will be all for now, but you can be sure that I will be in touch."

On his way home, Jim called Mae to make sure that she was okay. Of course, she wanted to know exactly what happened, but Jim knew the Feds must have tapped his phone, so he simply told Mae that everything was great. With that, Mae caught on and immediately changed the subject. "Dave called. He said that Susan had a baby boy. Hurry home, we must go to the hospital."

"I'll be right there, Mae. Be patient."

Jim took a cab right to the garage and got the station wagon. He picked Mae up at the door and drove to the hospital.

Arriving at the hospital, Jim and Mae were so excited to see Susan and Daniel, her new baby boy. With all of the commotion, Jim had almost forgotten about his afternoon with the U.S. Attorney. He had this overwhelming feeling of happiness in the hospital, but he knew that he needed to keep his fingers crossed because the future was still so uncertain. But he'd bet it would all turn out okay.

Conclusion

Now here's one for the road—a true story. One day, my neighbor told me about his family, born and raised on Long Island. His family went back over one hundred and fifty years when one area was known as Roosevelt Station of Long Island. There was nothing else on Long island but farms. Of course, at that time, all the farms had outhouses until the early 1920s.

In 1925, one farmer had a bathroom installed inside his house. After doing so, he still only used the outhouse. One day when his wife wanted to clean some spots off a pair of white gloves, she got a pan of gasoline to soak the gloves in. When she was finished, she poured the old gas down the hole in the outhouse. That evening, when her husband had to use the facility, he went out to the outhouse as usual. While sitting there, he decided to light up his pipe. After striking the match, he dropped the match down the toilet, causing a great explosion and blowing the outhouse to shreds. The farmer landed, out cold, on his back on the ground. His wife came running and screaming for help. When she got to her husband, she cradled him in her arms.

"What happened?" she asked when he woke up.

He looked up at her and said, "I guess that it was something I ate."

The author, Jim Bausch, and his wife, Mae, at the Roseland Ranch in 1983.